NAFTA on Second Thoughts

a plural evaluation

edited by
David R. Dávila-Villers

University Press of America,® Inc.
Lanham • New York • Oxford

University Press of America,® Inc.
4720 Boston Way
Lanham, Maryland 20706

12 Hid's Copse Rd.
Cummor Hill, Oxford OX2 9JJ

Printed in the United States of America
British Library Cataloging in Publication Information Available

Library of Congress Cataloging-in-Publication Data

NAFTA on second thoughts : a plural evaluation / edited by David R. Dávila-Villers.
p. cm.
1. Canada. Treaties, etc. 1992 Oct. 7. 2. Free trade—North America. 3. North America—Economic integration. I. Dávila Villers, David R.
HF1746.N3356 1998 382'.917 —DC21 98-9552 CIP

ISBN: 978-0-7618-1058-2

™The paper used in this publication meets the minimum requirements of American National Standard for information Sciences—Permanence of Paper for Printed Library Materials, ANSI Z39.48—1984

Contents

Part III

Introduction

Canada and Mexico are currently the first and third trade partners of the United States, respectively. At the present rate, bilateral trade between the US and Mexico shall grow in the next couple of years to overcome US trade with Japan. That is, the NAFTA will then be including the first and second largest trade partners of the US.

The NAFTA has originally been conceived as a trade agreement only. But, as experience has shown, integration is rich in spill-over effects. The NAFTA is no exception to the rule; witness of this are the NAFTA side agreements. Many important issues are presently urging to be included in the trilateral agreement (think of drug-trafficking, endangered species trafficking, labor mobility, energy, etc.). Since the NAFTA lacks the adequate framework to address them, those issues will remain important forces affecting the future of North America.

International integration is more than a choice. It is, above all, a global process that underlies such a choice made by governments. Tom Biersteker's chapter is to

> . . . suggest a conceptualization of what globalization is, illustrate changes underway in the thinking and operation of major institutional actors, briefly suggest why some of these changes are taking place, and consider their implications, with specific reference to North America.

Drawing on the economic side of the process, Biersteker contends that

> This change in the organization of production has been accompanied by a corresponding change in the organization of international finance.

In his view

> [Mexico and the US] are going to continue to share [. . .] and interdependent fate.

North American integration has advanced very quickly on many grounds. Notice on trade growth between the three countries has become customary in all major newspapers. Information on the financial realm is also crucial, although less easy to obtain. Eric Leroux has prepared a chapter aiming

> ... to assess the actual level of market access provided by Canada, the United States and Mexico in the banking sector.

Some interesting findings include

> . . . under present legislation, Canadian and Mexican banks are forbidden from doing in the United States what they are authorized to do in their own markets. When a US reform do occur they are to receive national treatment.

Leroux sustains that, while it is true that there has been progress in this area, this was not due to the NAFTA itself. In his own words

> . . . this further liberalization was not prompted by the NAFTA [trilateral cooperation did]

Interestingly enough, Ana Luisa Rojas reaches a similar conclusion, but from a different perspective. Ana Luisa Rojas's chapter is based on the performance of a textile company that has registered an export boom recently:

> we want to find out if NAFTA has brought substantial benefits to the company which is considered a successful company regardless of the current economic crisis.

Apparently, the NAFTA impact on the company is minor. More importance is attributed to other factors; such as the quotation of the peso. Ana Luisa claims

> . . . in an open economy only the industries that have high levels of productivity, an adequate market strategy, technology, the right products and the most efficient distribution channels will be able to survive as this will allow them to compete in the international market under a free trade scheme.

Ana Luisa's chapter closes the economic section of the book. However, as it was mentioned above, the NAFTA entails much more than its name can suggest. It might be asserted that, as Guy Claveau writes

> . . . the process of integration covers financial services, transportation, telecommunications, a policy on the environment, and all social and

> economic dimensions.

Claveau's chapter is on the role of educational institutions in the North American integration process. When it comes to cooperation, educational institutions can move real fast, as it has been happening. In the cultural realm, however, we might be contemplating the tip of the iceberg

> . . . the commitment of educational institutions and the acknowledgment of cultural dimensions and differences are only the beginning of the process.

Bussières represents Quebec's concerns for its cultural uniqueness. This preoccupation is heavy in implications for North America. From an ethical and realistic perspective, North America has no future if it does not engage in a strong defense of its rich multiculturalism, if it does not ensure the survival of its many different cultures.

In her chapter, Bussières reminds us

> Canada has always wanted to maintain protection to its cultural industries. This position is obviously motivated by the strength and the proximity of the US cultural industries and the fact that 75% of Canada share common language with the Americans.

> Trade liberalization for cultural industries, will be a top priority in future trade negotiations.

Serfaty's part revolves around cultural issues as well, but from a different stand-point. He introduces a very important element to be considered in all discussion of North American integration: the role of higher education institutions. In the case of Canada -Serfaty contends- universities might become increasingly active think-tanks in the foreign policy making process. In his own words,

> Canadian universities needed to make themselves more central to existing foreign policy concerns.

Interestingly, Serfaty found

> . . . Mexico ranked first as a priority region (or country) for future university links, outpacing even the very attractive Asia-Pacific connection. The US, on the other hand, was deemed third lowest priority area.

Thus, the role of Canadian universities in the North American integration process promises to be an expanding field for future research, as

> . . . the voice of Canadian universities may become more effective in the development of foreign policy.

Guillermo Rojas attacks one inescapable topic in US-Mexican relations: migration. Guillermo directs his analysis to dissect Pete Wilson's Proposition 187. In his own view

> . . . the illegal immigrants were the one working and paying taxes to provide the weekly revenue for the high-tech unemployed workers.

The relevance of the topic is here coupled with cunning insight. Guillermo finds underlying reasons to the California crisis, other than migration in itself. Pete Wilson's initiative has a very peculiar logic.

> [Proposition 187] targets racial groups, composed of non-voters in an act of political and cultural hypocrisy [for] the political dependency on the Pentagon [Washington defense contracts] and the federal budget cuts [are] the direct cause of the [Californian] deficit.

One of the darkest clouds in the NAFTA's horizon is its apparent inability to expand beyond the Mexican borders. In fact, the several candidates for accession had been confronted to the changing moods of US policy-makers; particularly congressmen. Renee Scherlen who has elsewhere written on the difficult (and unachieved) Chilean accession, offers herein a chapter on the possible alternatives for expansion. Thus, Scherlen indicates

> The subject of NAFTA enlargement has disappeared from public debate.

and offers

> . . . an assessment of how the silent treatment —developed in response

> to domestic pressures— affects US partners in NAFTA and Chile as well as the future of foreign policy coordination.

Hybel's chapter is also on foreign affairs and it supplements, in a way, the precedent author's assertions. Clearly, the United States has recently exhibited a notorious ineptitude in the face of a changing international system.

> . . . the end of the Cold War exposed not a hegemon incapable of designing a clear-minded policy, but a state forced to acknowledge its democratic roots in a world that had become noticeably more uncertain and complex than it had in nearly fifty years.

Besides, President Clinton, as Hybel says, had to develop an astute approach to foreign affairs. Despite the problems posed by the Republican control of Congress, the author can conclude

> [Clinton has been] successful at advancing his own foreign policy vision [which is defined by] the creation, protection, and enlargement of market democracies.

The concluding chapter addresses the main foreign policy disagreement among NAFTA partners. In this chapter, the editor of the book offers a quite provocative analysis of the Helms-Burton affair.

The author claims

> . . . the Cuban revolution was differently perceived in the three North American countries.

And far from accepting the present attitude of the US toward the island, Dávila assumes that

> Cuba is more likely to make democratic progresses and to complete its transition towards a mixed economy if the US lifts the embargo.

It was the failure of a long succession of administrations' foreign policies towards the Castro regime which prompted the US to strengthen the embargo. In other words

> . . . the Helms-Burton law is the US reaction to the economic recovery of Cuba in the post-Soviet era; it is an angry reaction to the Cuban success in attracting foreign partnership.

The end result of this issue may bring discord between the US and its two North American partners, with the consequent weakening of the agreement. Competing trading blocs, as the EU, might take advantage of the present dilemmas faced by the NAFTA. Because

> . . . what the US is doing is to break the unity of NAFTA while it faces a quite cohesive EU at the same time.

This concluding remark can help finally explain the title of the book: *NAFTA on Second Thoughts: a plural evaluation.*

Part I

Chapter I

Globalization and the North American Free Trade Agreement: Conceptual Changes within Major Institutional Actors and their Potential Implications *

Thomas J. Biersteker

The North American Free Trade Agreement is an important institutional achievement within the region, but it is by no means a unique development. Similar mevements toward greater economic integration and regional cooperation are underway in Europe, Asia, South America and Southern Africa. Even the former Soviet Union is reassembling itself in ways that occasionally approximate reintegration. At the same time, sub-national resistance and regional fragmentation have emerged within each of these regions (from Chiapas to Lombardy to Chechnya) and co-exist simultaneously and uneasly with tendencies toward greater regional integration. This fragmentation and the simutaneous impulse toward greater integration are not necessarily contradictory or the product of different forces. Rather, they may both be reactions to a larger, more significant development underway throughout the world today: the increasing globalization of institutional and individual behavior. Thus

* An expanded version of the theoretical portion of this paper was previously published in English in Oxford Development Studies, February 1998.

although NAFTA is significant in its own right, it is important to look at the agreement not in isolation, but in the larger context of globalization.

This short research will suggest a conceptualization of what globalization is, illustrate changes underway in the thinking and operation of major institutional actors, briefly suggest why some of these changes are taking place, and consider their implications, with specific reference to North America. While it will be not possible to reach definitive conclusions in the short space allotted, the conclusion will contain research hypotheses about the implications for North America, rather than research results. The latter will have to wait for more extensive study.

Conceptualizing globalization

Most of the popular discussion and scholarly literature characterize globalization in terms of the dramatic increase in the magnitude of international transactions- be they economic exchanges (increases in trade, financial, or investment flows), or technologically-driven transfer of information, ideas, and culture.[1] The macro-economic trends are indeed quite dramatic. For example, among the wealthiest countries (Europe, the U.S. and Japan), exports as a percentage of GDP more than doubled between 1960 and 1990 -from under 10% to over 20%. Thus, and increasing proportion of production from each OECD national economy is now intended for international markets. [2]

At the same time, the flow of foreign direct investment grew faster than trade through the 1980s, [3] and has expanded to include significant amounts of portfolio investment in the 1990s.[4] According to the IMF's latest World Economic Outlook, "net capital flows to developing countries averaged more than $130 billion a year during 1990-94, almost four times the flows during 1983-89."[5] Even more dramatic are recent changes in the structure of international finance. Although market segmentation continues, it is increasingly possible to trade in integrated global financial markets on a 24-hour a day basis. The stock of international bank lending rose dramatically during the 1980s, and world turnover in foreign exchange is now running at over $1.2 trillion per day!.

Much of the literature on globalization revolves around debates about the significance of these transactions, a discussion reminiscent of early 1970s arguments about the significance of the phenomenon of global interdependence. An alternative, and more useful, way to think about globalization is not in terms of increases in transactions, but as a basic change in the way in which major institutional actors think and operate. Changes in the thinking and modes of operation of institutions, in their ways of conceptualizing their mission, or in their basic rules and decision-making routines will in the end be more significant that dramatic increases in the magnitude of transactions. This is especially the case, if they involve a fundamental change from a local or national orientation toward a regional or global one.[6]

Changes in thinking and modes of operation of major institutional actors

Changes in thinking and modes of operation can be found in a variety on different types of institutions today. They are most visible in the changing structure of individual firms, but can also be seen in a variety of different non-governmental organizations (NGOs), within the foreign economic policy of individual states, and in major international institutions (particulary the international financial institutions).

There have been long debates about the existence of (or significance of) different trends in transactions involving firms, but globalization within firms is noticeable when they begin to change their basic modes of operation from a principal concern with national markets to a concern with planning, production, and servicing on a regional and global scale.[7] As Robert Reich has illustrated with his now classic example of a Japanese-owned multinational with a subsidiary in the U.S. seeking American government support against the unfair trading practices of an American-owned multinational exporting from East Asia, the idea of "national capital" is increasingly problematic.[8]

There is tremendous variation in the different organizational forms global production can take. The chain of production from research and development to final product distribution and servicing "can be articulated in different organizational and geographical ways."[9] In organizational terms, this means that research, production, and service might be contained within a single firm, or they might be sub-contracted in a variety of different ways to other firms. In geographical terms, while the location of research, production, or services might once have been contained within a single state, they are increasingly likely to be dispersed across different states. When you combine organizational change (the move to sub-contracting and multinational alliances) with increased geographical dispersal of activity (beyond the limits of a single state), it is possible to derive a virtually unlimited variety of different corporate forms.

Until recently, most of the transnational activity of large corporations was contained within a single entity which might take different organizational forms (from globally concentrated production within one country to host market production in different countries, product specialization for a regional market, or different forms of transnational vertical integration).[10] While different branches of this might be spread across different countries, they were all part of the same corporate entity. This was the classic model of the once national firm that became a multinational (or transnational) enterprise when it began to cross national boundaries in the postwar period. With the recent move toward sub-contracting and international business alliances, the picture has become far more complicated. At the outset, most firms began to sub-contract parts of their activity to firms within their home country in an effort to contain costs and remain competitive. Over time, however, more of this outsourcing was contracted with production sities dispersed across the globe. Figure 1 illustrates the emergence of the new organization of global production.

Figure 1

Org. Form	Geographical Dispersion of Enterprises	National (within one country)	Transnational (across national boundaries)
	Intra-firm	Most US firms (before 1950)	Classic MNCs (1960s and 1970s)
	Inter-firm	Sub-contracting within one country	Multinational Alliances and Transnational Sub-contracting (Nike-Benetton)

An ever growing number of firms has developed a network of global production locations and an investment strategy that spreads corporate risk (and tax liability) on a global scale. In industries like textiles, apparel, and footwear, more and more firms have embarked on flexible accumulation on a global scale, increasing their use of subcontracted production sites dispersed across the globe, shifting industrial organization to "just in time" delivery systems, pursuing flexible production, and introducing a variety of different types of "buyer-driven" commodity chains.[11] Companies like Nike or Benetton exemplify this new type of production organization.[12] These companies and firms like them are transforming consumption patterns worldwide by homogenizing global tastes and accelerating product turnover, introducing new product lines with ever shorter life spans (from eighteen to twelve months or even less). This tendency is not restricted to the largest corporations, but is increasingly found in small and medium sized firms as well.[13] Within the Mexican economy, much of this activity is concentrated in the maquiladora sector.

This change in the organization of production has been accompanied by a corresponding change in the organization of international finance.[14] There has been a major shift away from sharply demarcated national financial boundaries (with effective currency controls in place) toward increased financial liberalization, the elimination of currency controls, and an increased ease of cross-border financial transactions. This tendency toward financial liberalization (discussed more fully below) has facilitated the emergence of new financial actors (bond traders, currency traders, portfolio investors) who have developed global hedging strategies and now operate on an around the clock and around the globe basis. As a result, the emerging world financial market "is not comprised of linked national markets; in fact, it is not comprised of geographic locations at all. It is a network integrated through electronic information systems that entails'...more than two hundred thousand electronic monitors in trading rooms all over the world that are linked together"[15] This network has itself become a location of financial power and authority in the world, with and ability to reward contries that pursue policies it deems prudent, and to discipline those that pursue policies it deems unsustainable.[16] Few countries have experienced the force -or pace- of this increasingly globalized financial system as much as Mexico.

The combined effect of these changes in the organization of global production and finance has "rendered ambiguous" the traditional territorial imagenery of international political economy.[17] As John Ruggie has argued, we need to "unbundle" our concept of territoriality.[18] Control over flows and networks is becoming more important than hierarchical control over physical territorial space, as Timothy Luke demonstrated with reference to Kuwait (where royal family control over the flows of oil and wealth continued, even after the loss of control of all of the physical territory).[19] The emergence of the "region-state" —"natural" economic zones with integrated industrial investment and information systems that straddle national boundaries in an increasingly borderless world — is another manifestation of this blurring of traditional conceptions of territoriality.[20] The San Diego/Tijuana 'region-state" is a good illustration of this global phenomenon.

Globalization as a change in the mode of operation of institutional actors is not restricted to firms. There is also evidence of a shift in orientation within non-profit non-governmental organizations (or

NGOs). They are no longer just thinking globally and acting locally, but many are beginning to act globally as well. For example, environmental NGOs like Greenpeace have larger annual budgets than UNEP and are beginning to set agendas in international negotiations on global warming through the actions of their own "client states".[21] At the same time, many NGOs operating in the area of humanitarian intervention have been called upon to deliver services as part of international relief operations. Over ten percent of the total public development aid (approximately $8 billion) was disbursed by NGOs in 1994, "surpassing the volume of the combined UN system ($6 billion)" excluding the international financial institutions.[22] Finally, human rights NGOs have created issue networks that operate on a global scale, and have put effective pressure on states accused of violating individual and group rights, as well as on those states that might sanction them.[23] These networks have the power to draw attention to issues, to mobilize their transnational networks of support, and even to place issues on the national, regional, and global agenda. Local NGOs increasingly know how to tap into these networks, as we have seen in the case of opposition parties and human rights advocates in Mexico.[24]

While both firms and NGOs have changed, there has been an equally profound change in the way in which states organize and think about their relationship with the global economy in recent years. Most states have gone from an inward-oriented focus on the domestic economy (from import substitution industrialization or Keynesian counter-cyclical policies focused at the national level) to a preocupation with export orientation and national competitiveness. While states and their publics are still preoccupied with their national welfare (or standing), the means to attain advancement are increasingly perceived to be through greater participation in the world economy, not through insulation from it. This is a profund change, one I have described elsewhere as the "triumph" of neoclassical economic thinking in the developing world.[25] At the most general level, the economic ideas being pursued as policy throughout the world today include a reduction and transformation of state economic intervention, from production and distribution toward increased mediation and a redirection of regulation, an important revision of a principal component of Keynesianism in the postwar developing world.[26] John Williamson has described this change in discourse as the emergence of a "consensus" (or "universal convergence") around the objectives of fiscal discipline, adjustment of public expenditure priorities, tax reform, financial liberalization, exchange rate adjustment, privatization, deregulation, and support for property rights.[27] Again, no where has this policy shift been more dramatic than Mexico, long a parangon of economic nationalism, but a favorite model for neoliberal reformers since the mid-1980s.

The basic discourse of development has changed. The once fundamental opposition between capitalist West and socialist East no longer defines the boundaries of development discourse, and has been displaced by attention to a variety of forms of development within capitalism, along with some as yet inchoate alternatives from marginalized regions of the capitalist world economy. With the end of socialist development alternatives, the range of national development options has narrowed to choices within capitalism (even while our consciousness of the range of choice within capitalism has broadened appreciably). Thus, although there are national variations, there is apparently no going back from fundamental tenets of economic liberalization, especially in trade and financial liberalization. This has accelerated processes of trade liberalization and regional integration not just in North America, but on a global scale.

Another indication of the nature of change in foreign economic policy can be found within the OECD contries. Since the end of the Cold War, there has been a major shift in the rationale for giving foreign assistance. In the past, the principal motivation was for the purpose of strengthening foreign policy alliances or pursuing a variety of different moral goals. Today, one of the principal rationales for giving aid is to address regional or global problems, whether it involves the provision of new technologies (as called for in the ozone treaty) or for international strategies to deal with problems like global warming, the drug trade, or the scourge of AIDS.

Although the bulk of the discussion of the globalization of state policy falls within the realm of the international political economy, there is growing evidence of a globalization (as multilateralism) in the domain of national security policy, as well. Major states appear to be less inclined to undertake unilateral actions without some form of international backing, either from regional or global institution. This has been true even in the case of the U.S., when it obtained United Nations backing for the legitimation of its intervention in the Gulf War in 1990 and 1991 or its action in Haiti in 1994. At the same time, more and more states appear to be willing to accept the subcontracting of their military services to both regional and international organizations. U.S. forces have been placed under U.N. auspices in Macedonia; British, French, Dutch, aand Bangladeshi forces served under the U.N. in Bosnia; Russian troops presently served under U.S. command in the peacekeeping operations under OAU mandate in Liberia.

Finally, in addition to the globalization of firms, of NGOs, and of states policies, international institutions have altered their behavior and become increasingly intrusive into what have (at least in the recent past) been viewed as issues that are principally the prerogative of sovereign states. The Organization, and regional institutions have increased the frequency, the depth, and the scope of their interventions. While they have always thought and operated on a global scale, they have not gone as far into the historical domain of the "domestic" in the past. There is also an apparent acceptance of their intrusiveness on the part of most states: that is, the rethoric of states sovereignty is substantially muted at present (with the important recent exceptions of China and Nigeria).

The international Monetary Fund has introduced more extensive economic conditionalities with its system of "enhanced surveillance." The requierement that Mexico post its foreign exchange reserves on the Intenet on a weekly basis is indicative of this enhanced scrutiny. The World Bank has flirted with political conditionalities with the "new conditionality" it introduced in the early 1990s. The EBRD joined the Bank in this exercise, with the political conditions it imposed on the emerging democracies in east and central Europe. The World Bank has also introduced the idea of "green" conditionality, linking its assistance to enviromental protection. Not to be outdone, the new World Trade Organization has pressed the frontier of trade liberalization by becoming ever more intrusive into the historic domain og domestic politics. In the 1960s, the GATT began with a focus on lowering tariffs and moved progressively into non-tariff barriers during the 1970s and then to trade in services in the 1980s. The remaining challenge for trade liberalization is to move into changes in domestic labor and environmental policies. The U.S.-Japanese "structural impediments initiative" may have been one of the first illustration of this tendency. Finally, the growing willingness of the international comunnity to address, rather than ignore, emergencies within the borders of war-torn states (as indicated by the increased number of multinational peacekeeping operations under U.N. auspices during the last few years) is and illustration of the increased intrusiveness of international institutions in the political and milility realm.

Thus, evidence of globalization is visible in all of the major institutional actors on the world stage today. Fims, regardless of scale, have begun to go global, NGOs have begun to indentify and mobilize their networks across state boundaries, states have adapted their foreign economic and security policies, and international institutions have become far more intrusive into the realm of the "domestic" than they ever were in the past. Globalization as a change in mode of operation of major institutional actors has already gone quite far, and it is likely to have more far reaching implications than a simple incease in the volume of cross-border transaction. Before we can consider some of them, however, we need to address why globalization is taking place.

¿Why have these chages in modes of operation taken place?

In firms

1. Increasing competitiveness has forced firms to reduce costs through sub-contracting to other entities:

a. There are more national competitors for U.S. firms (which had no serious competition immediately after WWII, but increasingly has found itself pressured by Germany, Japan, the EU, and more recently by the NICs and China).

b. The pace at which technology is disseminated has accelerated significantly in recent years.

2. The complexity, cost, and risk of development of new technology have increased dramatically, prompting many firms to move into multinational alliances.

3. Most national markets are no longer large enough to be meaningful economic units. This is particulary pronounced in global financial markets, as financial firms have introduced hedging strategies on a global scale.

In NGOs

1. New information technology has made it possible view what is going on in dispersed places, create new (virtual) communities, and to mobilize publics throughout the world.

2. The bare outlines of a global civil society have begun to emerge in some issue domains (particularly in the areas of human rights and the environment).

In States

1. Policy convergence is the result of the drying up of non-conditional sources of finance during the 1980s. Financial crises explain the timing of the introduction of serious economic reform for most contries:

a. the debt crisis for Latin America in the early 1980s

b. raw material price decline for Africa at the same time

c. the oil price collapse in mid-1980s for the OPEC states
d. the Indian financial crisis in the early 1990s.

2. This policy shift has been reinforced in the 1990s by the fragility of the sources of finance that have emerged (largely portfolio investment). It is fragile because it can be moved so easily and with such devastating consequences.

3. The end of the Cold War and its long-term consequences for both the U.S. and the former Soviet Union have raised the costs of unilateral military action.

In International Institutions

1. The elimination of non-conditional sources of finance empowered the international financial institutions (IFIs) during the 1980s.

2. The policy shift toward market liberalization increased the number and range of instruments of influence at the disposal of the IFIs.

3. The end of the Cold War means that countries can no longer appeal for exemptions from conditionalities because of their "critical" role in some aspect of superpower conflict (neither can countries play one superpower off against another to increase their levels of foreign assistance).

Implications of globalization, with special reference to NAFTA

This discussion will be very preliminary, essentially a list of hypotheses that require investigation, not the reporting of research results.

From the globalization of firms and markets:

1. Locations of production can be readily shifted from one production site to another, keeping wage levels depressed. At the same time, the globalization of production spread production to locations in the developing world that otherwise might not have access to major markets in the OECD countries. Mexico could be a major beneficiary of the subcontracting of production activities across the border from the U.S. Evidence of the expansion of networks and subcontracting should be obtained, along with data on changes in wage demands.

2. As a general phenomenon, flexible accumulation tends to be

negative for women and minority populations, because those two groups tend to predominate in the markets for subcontracting to temporary labor (last hired, first fired). On the other hand, flexible accumulation can provide some formal sector employment experience for many that may prove useful for their subsequent employment at some future date.

3. Accelerated turnover and the constant introduction of new products with ever shorter product lives reinforces existing class divisions. Fewer and fewer people can afford to keep up with the pace of product change. However, it also keep markets growing and provides employment opportunities that might not otherwise have been created.

4. The globalization of finance constrains the policy aotonomy of all states, but especially states like Mexico. At the same time, the most recent (December 1994) financial crisis might have reinforced the tendency toward democratization in the country. The demand for openness and transparency in financial markets may translate into parallel demands for transparency in politics.

From the globalization of non-governmental organizations:

1. NGOs can give voice to groups traditionally repressed within states. Local NGOs can link up with their counterparts in more powerful countries (or with relatively easy eccess to international institutions). The environmental and human rights NGO communities have been particulary effective in this regard (on the "greening" of the World Bank and in bringing global attention to the plight of the Ogoni peoples of Nigeria).

2. While they can empower local NGOs, these groups are accountable only to their members and may have class and other biases.

3. Electoral monitoring NGOs have played a role in putting pressure on the Mexican government to liberalize politically.

From the globalization of policy thinking within states:

1.The short term costs of rapid economic reform are routinely negative. However, the medium to long term outcomes can be favorable, if certain institutional conditions are present (particularly if the reforms are implemented fully and maintained for an extended period of time).

2. In theory, rural populations should benefit from orthodox economic reforms, contributing to a very significant reduction in domestic inequality. However, there is surprisingly little reliable

economic evidence to confirm this point (i. e., geting the prices "right" and taking the state out of production and marketing is not sufficient, unless you have effective markets and other incentives in place).

3. Continued market-oriented economic reform will signal the end of the welfare state for the foreseeable future. At the same time, we may be entering a crisis of regulation, as increased inequality reduces the size of the mass market and narrows the base of support for policy reforms.

From the globalization tendencies within the international financial institutions:

1. The working out of the debt crisis taught us that the IFIs have much more leverage with debtor countries than with creditor banks. As Mexico and other heavily indebted countries learned, the bulk of the costs of debt was borne by the developing contries, and by the most marginal populations within them. However, conditionalities should be viewed within a bargaining framework (creditors rarely receive everything they want from debtors).

2. The asymmetries of power were stark in the 1980s, when the IFIs were the only source of finance for many contries. Moreover, they became powerful institutions which are not directly accountable to the countries that rely so heavily on their finance.

3. The increased intrusiveness of institutions like the World Trade Organization is likely to make it more difficult for most LDCs to access the markets of the EU, NAFTA, and East Asia. However countries located at the margins of the world's largest markets and in creasingly integrated with them (like Mexico) may benefit disproportionately from increased integration and policy harmonization.

¿Will Globalization Continue?

Theoretically, some of these tendencies toward globalization could be reversed — at least on a temporary basis — by states or other authorities interested in reasserting traditional ideas about sovereign authority.[28] Firms could be regulated, currency controls could be reestablished, NGOs could be repressed, international institutions could be ignored. But this would take a gargantuan collective effort. No single state could undertake and sustain the effort on its own.

Global technological changes are more or less permanent and have had an important effect on the emergence of new networks of production, on the globalization of financial markets, on the ability of

NGOs to pursue the struggle for the extension of rights or environmental protection, on the perceived need for UN intervention, and on the ability of international institutions to monitor activities within countries. It is increasingly difficult for governments to block their population's access to outside media influences. Portable satellite dishes, personal computers with fax modems, the Internet, and short wave radios confound centralized efforts to control communications and information flows. Even the recent Chinese (and American) attempts to put the genie of the Internet back in the bottle are likely to falter. In this respect, individuals and groups have gained considerably in power relative to the state, being limited only by money and ingenuity. Global technological advances have led to greater transparency, facilitated the transmission of norms and values, and helped to reinforce the shifting of authority to a growing number of locations outside the traditional territorial state.

Transnational networks have begun to displace the territorial state in the organization of global production, the distribution of global finance, the provision of emergency relief and assistance, the protection of individual and group rights, and the defense of the global environment. This development, facilitated by the technological change just described, has redefined state sovereignty (by reducing the number and range of authority claims made by states) and is likely to continue into the twenty-first century.

In the final analysis, the European experience with international integration may be illustrative when we begin to consider the reversibility of processes of regionalization and globalization in North America. There is little question that the process of integration in Europe has been halting in important respects (with major institutional achievements routinely followed by major setbacks in political support for continued integration).[29] However, the process of regional integration began with a limited focus on trade liberalization and has both widened and deepened — in spite of repeated declarations of its demise — over the course of nearly forty years. One reason for this continued progression may be that "once free market access is assured, it becomes much more difficult and expensive for governments to pursue other distortionary policies because they can be undermined by international trade."[30] As long as imports can move freely into the domestic market, a government will be restrained from reintroducing excessive regulation by its own firms, interested in maintaining their own competitive position.

Conclusion

Placing NAFTA in the context of globalization helps us understand both what the agreement has accomplished and what it cannot change. Some of the consequences attributed to NAFTA probably would have happened in any event, because they are the product of the globalization of major institutional actors. The recent expansion of the maquiladora sector would have occurred, albeit not at the same pace, as a result of the more general change in the organization of production and the emergence of region states along the border. The near doubling of the volume of total trade between the U.S. and Mexico that has taken place since 1990 is undoubtedly a product of the agreement, but it is worth noting that most of the increase took place before the agreement went into effect in 1994. The virtual explosion of portfolio investment into (and out of) the country in 1993 and 1994 (accounting for 90% of the net resource flows in 1993)[31] was undoubtedly facilitated by the presence of NAFTA, but did not rely on text of the agreement to guarantee access to the Mexican market. Similary, the cross-border activities of NGOs concerned with electoral reform, human rights, and the environment, do not depend on the agreement for their legitimacy. Finally, the shift in macro-economic policy and increased intrusiveness of international institutions predated the agreement and if anything, made NAFTA more likely.

Although some scholars have proclaimed "the end of geography,"[32] the simple fact that Mexico continues to share such a long border with the United States ("so far from God, so close to the United States...") means that the two contries are going to continue to share a similar interdependent fate. The blurring of the border in economic and cultural terms is likely to continue, with or without NAFTA. The North American Free Trade Agreement only determines the pace, and some of the manageability, of the process.

Notes

1 See for example, R.J. Barry Jones, **Globalization and Interdependence in the International Political Economy** (London and New York: Pinter Publishers, 1995).

2 Robert Wade, "Globalization and its Limits:Reports of the Death of the National Economy are Greatly Exaggerated," in Suzanne Berger and Ronald Dore (eds.) **Convergence or Diversity? National Models of Production and Distribution in a Global Economy** (Ithaca, NY: Cornell University Press, forthcoming 1995) p. 5 in manuscript form.

3 John Agnew, "The United States and American Hegemony," in P.J. Taylor (ed.) **The Political Geography of the Twentieth Century** (London: Belhaven Press, 1992).

4 Leslie Elliot Armijo, "Mixed Blessings? Foreign Capital Inflows and Democracy in Emerging Markets" Paper presented at the Workshop on Financial Globalization and Emerging Markets, Watson Institute for International Studies, Brown University, November 1995.

5 Reported in the **IMF Survey**, October 23, 1995, pp. 343-344.

6 Conceptualizing globalization as a basic change in the modes of thinking and operation of major institutional actors is closely related to dramatic increases in transactions. Indeed, it may be prompted by them. However, I think the two should be separated analytically for the purposes of this discussion.

7 Not all firms need to respond identically, for a significant change to be underway.

8 Robert Reich, **The Work of Nations** (New York: Knopf, 1991).

9 Peter Dickent, **Global Shift: The Internationalization of Economic Activity**, Second Edition (London: Paul Chapman Publishing Ltd., 1992) p. 225.

10 Ibid., p. 202.

11 Gary Gereffi, **"The Organization of Buyer-Driven Global Commodity Chains: How U.S. Retailers Shape Overseas Production Networks,"** in Gary Gereffi and Miguel Korzeniewicz (eds.) **Commodity Chain and Global Capitalism** (Westport CT: Greenwood Press, 1994).

12 Paul Knox and John Agnew, **The Geography of the World Economy**, Second Edition (London: Edward Arnold, 1994) p. 221.

13 Inmediately after the Mexican peso crisis of December 1994, a number of small and medium sized firms based in the state of Rhode Islan had cash flow problems associated whith the depreciation of the currency.

14 Benjamin J. Cohen, **"Phoenix Risen: The Resurrection of Global Finance, "World Politics 48** (January 1996) 268-96.

15 Stephen J. Kobrin, "Beyond Symmetry State Sovereignty in a Networked Global Economy," in John Dunning (ed.) **Governments, Globalization**

and International Business, (Oxford: Oxford University Press: forthcoming) p.20.

16 Thomas J. Biersteker, "The Changing Face of Sovereignty and the New Organization of Authority in the International System," paper prepared for the conference, Regional Integration and Democracy: The European Experience, Watson Institute for International Studies, Brown University, May, 1996.

17 Sthepen J. Rosow, "On the Political Theory of Political Economy: Conceptual Ambiguity and the Global Economy," **Review of International Political Economy**, 1 (Autumn 1994), 473-75.

18 John G. Ruggie, "Territoriality and beyond: problematizing modernity in international relations, "**International Organization**, 47,1 (Winter 1993) p.171

19 Timothy Luke, "The Discipline of Security Studies and the Codes of Containment: Learning from Kuwait, **Alternatives,** 16 (1991) 315-344.

20 Kenichi Ohmae, **The End of the Nation State: The Rise of Regional Economies**, (New York: Free Press, 1995) pp. 79-82.

21 Andrew Hurrell and Benedict Kingbury (eds.) **The International Politics of the Enviroment: Actors, Interes, and Institutions** (New York: Oxford University Press, 1992).

22 Leon Gordenker and Thomas Weiss, Pluralizing Global Governance: Analytical Approaches and Dimensions" in their edited book, **NGOs, the UN, and Global Governance** (Boulder, CO.: Lynne Rienner Publisher, 1996) p.25. They argue that 25% of US assistance is channeled through NOGs and that while he has attending the Social Summit in Copenhagen, U.S. Vice President Al Gore pledged to increase that amount to 50% by the end of the decade.

23 Kathryn Sikkink, "Human rigths, principle issue networks, and sovereignty in Latin America," **International Organization**, 47, 3, Summer 1993 (pp. 411-441).

24 Jorge Castaneda has decried how opposition parties in Mexico have tried to get media coverage in the U.S. press in order to put transnational pressure on the PRI to open up the political process in Mexico (in a lecture at the Center for International Studies, University of Southern California, Los Angeles, March 1992).

25 Thomas J. Biersteker, "The Triumph' of Liberal Economic Ideas in the Developing World," in Barbara Stallings (ed.) **Global Change, Regional Response** (Cambridge University Press, 1995).

26 Thomas J. Biersteker, "Reducing the Role of the State in the Economy: A Conceptual Exploration of IMF and World Bank Prescriptions," **International Studies Quartely** 34, 4 (December 1990): 488.

27 John Williamson, **The Progress of Policy Reform in Latin America** (Washington, D.C.: Institute for International Economics, 1990), p.59.

28 As suggested in the introduction to this research note, there are strong countervailing resistances to integration and pressures for local autonomy in many parts of the world today.

29 This may in part be the product of the historical pattern of decoupling the institutional commitment to further integration from the experience of the stresses of adjustment in Europe. See L. Alan Winters, "What Can European Experience Teach Latin America about Integration? "Paper presented at the Seminar on The Hemispheric and Regional Integration in Perspective, Santafe de Bogota, 1-3 November 1995, organized by the Departamento Nacional de Planeación, República de Colombia, p. 11.

30 Ibid., p. 15.

31 Armijo, "Mixed Blessings," Table 7A.

32 John Stopford and Susan Strange, **Rival States, Rival Firms: Competition for World Market Shares** (Cambridge: Cambridge University Press, 1991) p. 40.

Chapter II

Evolution of banking legal frameworks in Canada, the United States and Mexico under NAFTA's chapter 14 on financial services

Eric Leroux

Introduction

The North American Free Trade Agreement (NAFTA), which came into force on January 1st, 1994, contains, as we all know, a specific chapter covering the financial services sector (chapter 14). One of the objectives in regard of this agreement on financial services was obviously for each country to obtain, on a non-discriminatory basis, a better access to the financial markets of its counterparts. Such access depends directly on the existing national legal framewwork in each country involved. As a result of NAFTA negotiations in the financial services sector, the level of market access offered by Canada, the United States and Mexico was established on January 1st, 1994, with no possibility of going back; that is to say, that a Party to the agreement could not impose new restrictions to the entry and operations on its territory of other Parties' financial institutions; it could only liberalize further its financial regulation in accordance with the principles established in NAFTA's chapter 14, among them the national treatment principle, thus offering better market access to the financial institutions of other Parties.

The purpose of this exposé is to assess the actual level of market access provided by Canada, the United States and Mexico in the banking sector. To accomplish this, one must look at the changes that occurred in the legal banking frameworks of those three countries since the entry into force of NAFTA, although we can immediately say that most of them have taken place during 1995.

Developments in the United States

The United States has been struggling for a long time to reform its financial system, to liberalize it and make it more efficient, in particular in the banking sector. This can be explained by a number or reasons, not the least being the fact that legislative power in this particular sector is divided between federal and State authorities, thus rendering quite difficult to achieve a complete reform of the American banking system.

When NAFTA was negotiated, the obstacles that were viewed as impediments to market access in the United States were those related to interstate banking and branching and the institutional barriers prohibiting, as a general rule, a bank from conducting insurance and investment activities.[1] At a time of financial internationalization and regulation (or re-gulation), when a majority of countries have undertaken substantial reforms in order to eliminate institutional barriers and provide financial institutions with a posibility to be more efficient on a geographical scale, these restrictions were considered burdensome and unnecessary. They were however maintained by the United States in NAFTA, with the assurance that should they be eliminated or modified, Canadian and Mexican banks would have the rigth to be treated on the same footing as American banks under NAFTA's section 1405 which stipulates the national treatment principle. Some liberalization has occurred with respect to interstate banking and branching, but the banks will still have to wait before being able to fully enter the insurance and investment sectors.

The Riegle-Neal Interstate and Branching Efficiency Act of 1994

On September 29th, 1994, was enacted the Riegle-Neal Interstate and Branching Efficiency Act, a federal act with the purpose of providing banks with more possibilities to conduct activities throughout the U.S territory through subsidiaries or branches.[2]

Prior to the enforcement of this act, the legislative landscape with respect to interstate branching and banking in the United States was as follows: national banks and State member banks (members of the

Federal Reserve System) were forbidden from establishing branches in different States by virtue of the McFadden Act.[3] Thus it was practically impossible for a bank to develop a branch network throughout the U.S. territory as this is possible in Canada or Mexico for example. Moreover, a bank holding company could not acquire a bank located outside its home State -the State in which it had its principal operations - unless such operation was permitted by the host State - the State where the acquisitions are sought. As for many years quite a number of States prohibited such acquisitions on their territory, whether in an absolute manner or on a discriminatory basis, the posibility for a bank holding company to have subsidiaries in different States across the country was also limited.

Foreign banks were subjected to a similar scheme by virtue of the Internacional Banking Act of 1978,[4] a federal act providing national treatment to foreign banks operaiting in the United States. The possibilities for Canadian and Mexican banks to extend their U.S. operations on a geographical scale were therefore quite limited.

That was the existing situation when NAFTA was adopted. Now, with the Riegle-Neal Interstate Banking and Branching Efficiency Act, a bank holding company[5] is able, since October 1995 and with Federal Reserve Board approval, to acquire a bank located outside its home State, whether or not the host State's legislation permits. Moreover, since the enactment of the Riegle-Neal Interstate Banking and Branching Efficiency Act on September 29th, 1994, national and State banks can open branches outside their home State (de novo branching) so long as a host State's legislation authorizes it.[6] Finally, commencing June 1 st, 1997, national and State banks will be authorized to merge across State lines, thus creating a sole institution with branches, unless the States in which are located the banks involved have, prior to that date, enacted legislation forbidding such operations. Such mergers will also be possible prior to June 1 st, 1997, provided that States involved enacted legislation to that effect. As of January 1 st, 1996, only the State of Texas had enacted opting-out legislation prohibiting such mergers with banks located on its territory, and 19 other States had adopted early opt-in legislation.[7] Thus it seems likely that there will exist a truly national banking system in the United States by mid-1997. Banks should be able to set up efficient national branch networks throughout most of the U.S. territory, and many of them are getting prepared buying other banks which will ultimately be transformed into branches when it is permitted to do so.

As we can see, this new federal legislation is a good step toward liberalizing the banking business geographically speaking, although the State legislatures still play a determinant role over the final outcome. Under NAFTA's section 1405, Canadian and Mexican banks must be afforded de facto national treatment with respect to these legal modifications, which means in accordance with the wording of NAFTA "equal competitive opportinities" as compared to American banking institutions. The act itself appears to provide national treatment to foreign banks in that they are authorized to establish branches outside their home State either by way of acquisition or de novo branching. That means that a priori , Canadian and Mexican banks will therefore be able to operate through branches throughout the U.S. territory so long as it is permitted for U.S. banking institutions to do so.

One will have to see though how the new legislation is "in fact" applied to Canadian and Mexican banks to know if the de facto-national-treatment criteria stipulated in NAFTA is indeed complied with. Moreover, we must emphasize that the International Banking Act imposes on foreign banks a requirement to establish in the United States an insured banking subsidiary in order to be able to accept or maintain domestic retail deposit accounts having balances of less than US$ 100 000.[8] What this practically means is that for a Canadian or a Mexican bank to conduct retail banking activities and fully take advantage of the new opportunities with respect to interstate branching, it must have a separately-capitalized subsidiary on the U.S. territory.[9] This is to say, in the case of Canada's major banks for example, that for the moment there is only the Bank of Montreal which is in a position to fully benefit from the opportunities created by the legislation, as it is the only major Canadian bank with a U.S. subsidiary (Harris Bankcorp in Chicago).

One can also ask what this new act means with regard to NAFTA's section 1403.3 which specifies that when the United States will permit commercial banks of other Parties located on its territory to expand through subsidiaries or direct branches into substantially all of the U.S. market, the Parties "shall review and asess market access provided by each Party... with a view to adopting arrangements permitting investors of another Party to choose the juridical form of establishment of commercial banks". This clearly refers to the requeriment of the subsidiary form, as compared to the branch form, imposed by Canada and Mexico to American banks that want to operate on their territories.[10]

Indeed, U.S. banks are seeking the right to establish themselves on foreign soils through branches rather than through subsidiaries, because the latter form is much more expensive and burdensome for it means that the foreign bank must set up a separately-capitalized corporation which has more limited lending powers. By virtue of

NAFTA's section 1403.3, the United States have asked its NAFTA associates for a review of market access so that U.S. banks could establish themselves on their territories by way of branches rather than trough subsidiaries. Mexico is in fact exempted of those consultations because of a reservation included in NAFTA through annex 1403.3.

Canada, for its part, responded that the implementation of the Riegle-Neal Interstate Banking and Branching Efficiency Act is still in a too-early phase to consider whether or not the condition set forth in NAFTA's section 1403.3 is being fulfilled by the United States. The matter shall therefore be looked at more seriously when the implementation of the Riegle-Neal Interstate Banking and Branching Efficiency Act is completed in June 1997. A reform of the Canadian financial system is expected for that specific year, and Canada will then consider whether or not to eliminate the above-mentioned requirement.

One must however emphasize that NAFTA only provides for consultations on the matter, and therefore there is no obligation on the part of Canada to afford such a branching right to U.S. banking institutions.

Institutional barriers: the Glass-Steagall legislation

An other important item on the U.S. banking agenda is the institutional barriers issue. In virtue of the *Glass-Steagall Act*[11] of 1933 and the *Bank Holding Company Act*[12] of 1956, a banking institution is presently forbidden, as a general rule, from conducting investment and insurance activities, this being in sharp contrast with what exists, subsequently to major financial reforms and through different structures, among others in the European Union, Canada and Mexico.

At the beginning of 1995, there seemed to be a new impulse toward a reform of the institutional barriers issue. Three approaches were considered: one was to eliminate the barriers between commercial banking and investment activities;[13] another was to eliminate all institutional barriers; i.e., to allow banks affilliate with securities firms, insurance companies;[14] the third one, supported by the Clinton Administration, favored the affiliation of banks with securities firms and insurance companies.

The proposal that finally went forward is the one that would essentially allow banks to affiliate with securities firms. The bill that is still presently considered would allow affiliations between those types of institutions but only through holding companies, which is a form disliked by banks because it is much more burdensome.[15] Banks would rather prefer to be allowed to pursue investment activities directly, in accordance with the universal bank structure. Moreover, due to insurance industry pressure, the proposed bill contains provisions that would impose a five-year ban on the Office of the Comptroller of the Currency's ability to expand bank insurance activities. This measure is also constested by banking institutions and the insurance industry will not let the proposal pass without it.[16]

The institutional-barriers-reform issue is thus blocked in Congress and now that we have entered into an election year, significant action with respect to such an important and debated matter is unlikely. Therefore, it seems that one will have to wait till at least 1997 before this issue can be really re-considered.

What this means for Canadian and Mexican banks is that they continue to be forbidden from doing in the United States what they are authorized to do into their own markets. When a U.S. reform do occur however, maybe in 1997 or 1998, they are assured to receive the same benefits from it than U.S. institutions by virtue of NAFTA's section 1405 on national treatment. As concerns the particular case of Mexican financial groups which conducted, prior to NAFTA, banking and securities activities in the United States, one must remember that they must comply with the Glass-Steagall legislation forbidding the joint conduct of those activities within a period of 5 years from the date of acquisition of the securities firm.[17]

Developments in Canada: the financial reform expected for 1997

The Canadian banking legal framework has not changed much since the entry into force of the NAFTA in 1994. Prior to this agreement, provincial and federal authorities had undertaken substantial reforms mainly to eliminate the institutional barriers between the different segments of the financial system. Banks were permitted to acquire insurance companies, securities firms and trust and loan companies, which they did quite rapidly. The portrait of the Canadian financial system thus changed considerably in a few years, with the formation of major financial groups controlled by banks.[18]

Foreign banks were afforded the benefit of this deregulation. And with the adoption first of the Free Trade Agreement between Canada and the United States on January 1st, 1989, and later the NAFTA,[19] American and Mexican banks were also freed from discriminatory restrictions in the Canadian banking sector, that is to say the limit to foreign participation in Canadian banks[20] and the total capital limit applicable to foreign bank subsidiaries.[21] American and Mexican banks were thus enjoying, on a fairly nondiscriminatory basis, large access to a recently liberalized financial market. The only restriction left in debate during the NAFTA negotiations is the one to which we have already referred and concerns the obligation for foreign banks to establish themselves in Canada through subsidiaries rather than through branches. As we said, this is a matter that will probably be considered during the 1997 Canadian financial reform.

This reform is already on its way and although it is difficult at this point to predict the exact outcome of it, one can say that the main issue in debate is wether or not banks should be authorized to sell insurance services through their branch networks.[22] As we have already mentioned, the banks have gained, during the last federal financial reform wich occurred in 1992, the right to acquire insurance companies and to operate them through the form of a subsidiary. However, this does not include the right for banks to sell insurance products directly, and this is what is now considered with respect to that forthcoming reform. The major Canadian banks, which are already dominant into the financial market and reported record profits in 1995 ($CAN 5.18 billion for the Big Six Banks[23]), are generally more efficient than insurance companies and want to be authorized to use their vast branch networks to provide insurance products directly to the consumers.[24] Insurance companies do not consider it to be appropiate though, especially since the competition is already fierce in an already overcapacitated industry and many of them are experiencing difficult times.[25]

Market access afforded by Canada to American and Mexican banks has therefore not really changed since the entry into force of NAFTA. One must however emphasize that as the Canadian banking market is already largely liberalized and opened to foreign banks, there is not much to expect in this regard. Should modifications nevertheless occur in 1997, U.S. and Mexican banks are assured to be treated equally i.e. on a de facto national treatment basis[26] with respect to any new legal framework coming out of such modifications.

Developments in Mexico: the financial crisis and the further opening of the banking market

The major component of the financial services agreement included in NAFTA was obviously the opening of Mexico's financial market to American and Canadian financial institutions. When NAFTA was negotiated, Mexico was still in the process of reorganizing and restructuring its financial system following the privatization of the banking system at the beginning of thr 90's. It needed time before completely opening its market to foreign investors and meeting competition from U.S. and Canadian financial institutions. Therefore, as we all know, there was a six-year transition period negotiated, ending on January 1st, 2000 and during which American, Canadian and also U.S. and Canadian subsidiaries of other countries'financial institutions were authorized to gradually penetrate the Mexican market through subsidiaries subjected to capital limits.

The advent of major economic and financial crises following the peso devaluation in December 1994 has however forced the Mexican authorities to modify this. The crisis especially put Mexican banks in a perilous situation, with severe problems of lack of capital, and the Mexican government, as part of its rescue plan, opened further its banking market to foreign investors so that needed capital could be injected into troubled institutions.

On February 16, 1995, the following modifications entered into force in the banking sector: the foreign participation limit in Mexican banks passed to 49% of equity from 30%, with an individual limit of 20%.[27] NAFTA banking institutions, that is to say Canadian and American banks as well as Canadian or American banking subsidiaries of non-NAFTA countries, are also permitted to take control of Mexican banks, subject to an authorization from the Secretaría de Hacienda y Crédito Público (Department of Finance).[28] However, the latter cannot authorize the acquisition of a Mexican bank if its capital exceeds 6% of aggregate banking capital in Mexico, thereby putting out of reach from foreign acquisition the top three Mexican banks, Banamex, Bancomer and Banca Serfín, which together account for more than half of total banking assets in Mexico. Moreover, total capital of Mexican banks acquired must not represent more than 25% of aggregate banking capital in Mexico.[29]

These legal changes mean that through "acquisitions", NAFTA banks are authorized to take a larger share of the Mexican banking market than what is stipulated in NAFTA. Indeed, one must remember that under NAFTA, Canadian and American bank subsidiaries in Mexico are subjected, during the six-year transition period, to a 1.5% individual capital limit and a 8-15% global capital limit (starting at 8% on January 1st, 1994, and incremented annually until reaching 15% on January 1st, 1999). Moreover, one must also remember that NAFTA specifies that after the end of the transition period, a 4% individual capital limit is to be applied on a permanent basis with respect to "acquisitions" of Mexican banks, and the total capital of NAFTA bank subsidiaries can be freezed for a period of three years not extending after January 1st, 2007, if it reaches 25% of total banking capital in Mexico. Those limitations still apply in regard of the establishment of Mexican subsidiaries by NAFTA banks, but in the particular case of the acquisition of Mexican banks by such foreign institutions, the limits applicable are the above-mentioned 6% and 25% limits.

Henceforth, what occurred was that Mexico simply renounced to certains right specified in NAFTA with respect to a particular situation: the acquisition of Mexican banks. Otherwise, the limits negotiated in NAFTA continue to apply. In accordance with NAFTA, the 6% limit will be applied on a permanent basis and the 25% one will end on January 1st, 2000, after which date the above-mentioned three-year-freeze provision will apply normally.

Those new opportunities have not attracted many foreign investors though. Indeed, during 1995, there is only the Spanish bank Bilbao Vizcaya which, through its Portorican subsidiary, took control of a mexican bank, Mercantil Probursa.[30] Among the reasons for this lack of interest from foreign banks, one can certainly mention the state of the Mexican economy and its desastrous consequences on the domestic banking business.[31] A great number of Mexicans were unable to repay their debts to the banks, thereby increasing enormously bank's non performing loans rate. By the end of January 1996, that rate was still evaluated by Mexican authorities near 17%.[32] One can also refer to the lack of transparency with respect to banks' financial statements. Indeed, one criticism that has especially surged in this regard is the indequacy of accounting rules presently used to establish banks' non-performing loans rate, the result being that the real rate, which is more likely to be near 30% on average, is being occulted.[33] It has however been announced that those rules will be changed in accordance with those used in the United States beginnning on January 1st, 1997.[34]

During 1995, foreign banks have thus mainly concentrated on developing their own operations in Mexico through representative offices or subsidiaries. Meanwhile, the Mexican government had to rescue by itself the banking system, through programs such as the PROCAPTE[35] and the FOBAPROA,[36] in order to prevent banks from falling down, which represented a systemic risk. This governmental rescue is however not being without tremendous costs. Indeed, at the beginning of the current year, it was estimated that the rescue programs set up by the government had cost some US$ 15 billion, which is already more than what the same government received 4 years ago from the privatization of the banking system (US$ 13.55 billion).[37]

1996 could however bring more foreign investment into the Mexican banking system. At the end January 1996, it was announced that Bank of Nova Scotia, a Canadian bank which already had a minority parcitipation of 8.5% in Grupo Financiero Inverlat,[38] would acquire a controlling share in this financial group, thus taking control of Banco Inverlat,[39] a major Mexican bank representing near 6% of the total banking capital in Mexico.[40] It was also announced that serious negotiations were going on between Bancomer and Bank of Montreal, another Canadian Bank, as to the taking of a 12% participation by the latter in Bancomer, such operation apparently representing a US$ 500-million capital injection into the Mexican bank.[41] This could be the sign that foreign institutions are regaining confidence with respect to Mexico and its medium to long-term perspectives in the banking sector. It is also a good sign for the Mexican government which cannot be forever the principal rescuer for the banks.[42]

Conclusion

In conclusion, market access changes have taken place in the United States and Mexico since the entry into force of NAFTA.

With regard to the United States, the new legislation adopted during 1994, the Riegle-Neal Interstate Banking and Branching Efficiency Act, will gradually help transform the portrait of the U.S. banking system on the geographical scale. Banks are struggling for more effiency and this goes with a U.S. banking system with a less burdensome regulatory framework. For many years we have witnessed a trend toward consolidation in the U.S. banking sector and the Riegle-Neal Interstate Banking and Branching Effiency Act goes in that direction. With respect to NAFTA and the market access issue, one must now look closely at the final implementation of this legislation by federal and State authorities and at the compliance with the de facto-national—treatment obligation stipulated in NAFTA. and to which are entitled Canadian and Mexican banks.

Another major step toward more efficiency and further liberalization with respect to the U.S. banking system would have been a reform of the old Glass-Steagall legislation, but this was not reached and it is unlikely that it will till at least or 1998.

Mexico, for its part, had promised in 1995 to open further, ahead of time shall we say, its banking market to foreign banks, in particular NAFTA ones. The main thing about this new liberalization is that NAFTA banks can now acquire any of the existing Mexican banks but the three largest, which are Banamex, Bancomer and Serfín. Apart from the acquisition of Mercantil Probursa by Spanish bank Bilbao Vizcaya in 1995 and the still unofficial (when this text was written) acquisition of Inverlat by the Canadian Bank of Nova Scotia this year, such measure did not attract many foreign investors primarily because of the state of the Mexican economy. Thus Mexican banks had to be rescued in large part by their government and their recovery undoubtedly starts with the Mexican economy getting better.

One could finally ask what was the role played by NAFTA's chapter 14 on financial services since its entry into force. One could perhaps say that no significant role was played, for those developments occurred independently of NAFTA; in other words, this further liberalization was not prompted by NAFTA. This could however be minimizing the importance of the coordination and cooperation achieved between the three countries mainly through NAFTA's Financial Services Committee. It would also be forgetting that NAFTA is above all a mean to protect the access enjoyed by one country's institutions to another country's market by way of a set of obligations like the national treatment or the impediment to impose new restrictions to another Party's institutions[43], and that as such, NAFTA's chapter 14 on financial services does play a role in that it serves as a guaranty for each country's institutions. The fact is though that the strength of such protection still has not really been put to the test in the financial services sector; no serious problems occurred so far with respect to that part of NAFTA, hopefully shall we say. No doubt however that with the continuation of the process of financial integration in North America, this should not always be the case.

Notes

1 See E. LEROUX, *Le Libre-échange Nord-américain et les Services Financiers*, Montréal, Les Editions Yvon Blais Inc., 1995, pp. 10-15, 33-43, 99-101.
2 Pub. L. No. 103-328, 108 Stat. 2338.
3 12 U.S.C § 36 (1988).
4 12 U.S.C. §§ 3101-3108 (1988); this federal act was adopted in 1978 in order to subject foreign banks to a regulation scheme similar to the one applicable to U.S. banking institutions.
5 The act specifies an "adequately-capitalized and adequately-managed bank holding company".
6 For an analysis of this new act, see: M. A. INDICK, S. M. KINI, The Interstate Banking and Branching Efficiency Act: New options, New Problems, (1995) 112-2 *Banking Law Journal* 100; S. C. STOCK, M. E. PLOTKIN, "A Summary of the Riegle-Neal Interstate Banking and Branching Efficiency Act of 1994", (1994) 10 J.I.B.L. 402.
7 "Multistate Pacts Seek to Help State Banks on Interstate Branching", (1996) 155-1 *Banking Policy Report*, pp. 4ff.
8 *International Banking Act*, 12 U.S.C. § 3104(c) (1988).
9 This is to compare with the fact that it is generally possible for a foreign bank to have only branches in the United States.
10 This requirement is imposed for prudential concerns. Indeed, a subsidiary is a separate corporation established in accordance with laws of the State of establishment. It is therefore entirely subjected to the laws and the regulatory authorities of that State. On the contrary, a branch is a mere extension of the same corporation into another State. Thus one can say that it is only partially subjected to the laws and regulatory authorities of the State where it is established, therefore making it more difficult for the latter to control the activities of this type of institution.
11 12 U.S.C. §§ 24, 78, 377, 378 (1988).
12 12 U.S.C. §§ 1841-1850 (1988).
13 Supported by Jim Leach, newly-appointed chairman of the House Banking Committee.
14 Supported by Senate Banking Committee Chairman Alfonse M. D'Amato and Richard Baker, senior member of the House Banking Committee.
15 *Financial Services Competitiveness and Regulatory Relief Act of 1995*, H.R. 2520. Jim Leach, House Banking Committee chairman, is expected to bring this bill to the House floor in March or April 1996.

16 "Year in Review", (1996) 15-1 *Banking Policy Report* 6ff.

17 Annex VII, schedule of the United States, section C.

18 See E. LEROUX, op. cit., pp. 5-10.

19 The aplication of the Free Trade Agreement between Canada and the United States has been suspended since the entry into force of NAFTA on January 1st, 1994.

20 The 25% limit applicable with respect to Schedule I banks, which are the major Canadian banks, as opposed to to Schedule II banks, which generally are subsidiaries of foreign banks.

21 Since the entry into force of the Agreement Establishing the World Trade Organization on January 1st, 1995, Canada has also eliminated those restrictions with respect to other signatories' banks. This agreement can be found in SECRETARIAT DU GATT, Résultats des négociations commerciales multilatérales du cycle d'Uruguay: textes juridiques, Génève, Secrétariat du GATT, 1994.

22 J. PARRIDGE, K. HOWLETT,"Watchdog to Aid Reform of Financial Laws", The Globe & Mail, December 1st, 1995, B1 and B8.

23 Royal Bank of Canada, Canadian Imperial Bank of Commerce, Bank of Montreal, Bank of Nova Scotia, Toronto-Dominion Bank and National Bank of Canada.

24 Analysts say the banks could grab 30% of an open insurance market.

25 One can remember the collapse of Confederation Life Insurance Co. in 1994, a 123-year-old institution with $CAN 19 billion in assets, which greatly affected consumer and capital market confidence.

26 Section 1405 of NAFTA.

27 *Diario Oficial de la Federación*, Tomo CDXCVII, No. 11, México, D.F., 15 de febrero de 1995.

28 Idem; W. ACWORTH, "Foreigners Allowed up to 51% of Mexican Banks; but Banamex, Bancomer and Serfin Seen Out of Reach", (1995) 8-5 LCD Debt Report/Latin American Markets 6.

29 *Diario Oficial de la Federación, supra.*

30 The acquisition occurred in June 1995. Bilbao Vizcaya paid about US$ 350 million for a 70% participation in Multibanco Probursa, a financial group controlling the Multibanco Mercantil Probursa bank: H. RICE, "Treading Lightly South of the Border", U.S. Banker, September 1995, pp. 42 ff.; "Puerto Rico Offshore Banking Gets a Boost: BBV International Investment Served as Transfer Agent for BBV's Purchase of Mexico's Grupo Financiero Probursa", Caribbean Business, June 1995, 11.

31 Which makes perspectives of penetrating the retail banking business not very attractive.

32 G. TORRES, "La banca zarandea aún más la débil economía de México", Reforma, 25 de enero de 1996, 26A.

33 G. TORRES, op. cit., 26A.

34 M. VAZQUEZ, "Cambian criterios contables", Reforma, 23 de enero de 1996, 1A.

35 Programa de Capitalización Temporal (Program of Temporary Capitalization).

36 Fondo Bancario de Protección al Ahorro (Banking Fund for the Protection of Investment).

37 E. RIVERA, M. E. GARCIA, "Sube costo fiscal bancario", Reforma, 18 de enero de 1996, 20A.

38 Bank of Nova Scotia first acquired a 5% participation in 1992, and subsequently increased the latter to 8.5%.

39 M. VAZQUEZ, "Pierde control Inverlat", Reforma, 31 de enero de 1996, 1A.

40 Data from the Comisión Nacional Bancaria y de Valores show that on June 1995, Banco Inverlat represented 5.8% of total banking capital in Mexico.

41 E. RIVERA, J. VASQUEZ, "Elogian negociación de Bancomer", Reforma, 25 de enero de 1996, 20A.

42 Some people have already talked of a "re-nationalization" of banks, due to the amount of capital injected so far into banks by the Mexican government. At the end of 1995, the government had injected near US$ 5.42 billion into nine Mexican banks: "No hay dinero para capitalizar bancos", Reforma, 23 de diciembre de 1995, 17A.

43 Cf. section 1409 of the agreement.

Chapter III

NAFTA and Economic Progress: the case of Polifil Industries

Ana Luisa Rojas

I have been invited to present at this congress Polifil's position as a textile export industry during the first two years of the North American Free Trade Agreement. The aim of this paper is to show the effects (either positive or negative) that the treaty has brought about since its implementation in 1994.

In regards to the countries involved in the agreement, it is important to mention that for the moment, Polifil is exporting only to the USA. About 80% of its exports are destined to this country.

The key questions that I hope this paper will answer are:

- In regards to the import and export procedures, did time of response diminish? Have administrative procedures changed at all? In other words, has the treaty made things easier for Polifil in respect to its foreign trade activities with the United States?
- Concerning technology upgrading, has NAFTA made access to loans for new machinery easier?
- About the performance of the company as a successful exporter, did sales to the United States increase quantitatively? that is, in terms of money and exported tons?.

On the whole we want to find out if NAFTA has brought substantial benefits to the company which is considered a successful company regardless of the current economic crisis.

Before answering the above questions I would like to talk a little bit about Polifil Industries mentioning the products that we produce and also the countries to which we are currently exporting, after doing this I will then focus in our export relations with the United States.

Industrias Polifil S.A. de C.V.

Polifil Industries is a factory dedicated to the manufacture of mass pigmented polypropylene fibers and yarns.[1]

Polifil started to export yarn and fibers in the late 1970's. By the end of the 1980's Polifil exported to the following countries: The USA, Canada, Guatemala, Costa Rica, England, Belgium, Sweden, Japan, Malaysia, Thailand, Singapore, Taiwan, Hong Kong, Australia and New Zealand. In February 1989, SECOFI awarded Polifil the ALTEX Certificate.[2]

Polifil has managed to attain recognition as a competitive industry at world level in part due to its high quality products and also to technology upgrading which, in turn, have given it the ability to maintain its position in the international market for the last twenty years.[3]

The yarn and fibers that Polifil produces are high quality products that meet the accepted domestic and international standards. It offers a wide range of textures and colours.[4] It counts with a production capacity of around 12,000 tons per year. Approximately 65% of Polifil's production is exported. [5] Its products are used in industries such as tapestry, automobile upholstery and carpeting. For the last five years, the export markets in order of importance have been The United States (83 %), Australia (10 %), Central and South America (6.8 %) and a few countries in Europe (0.18 %). The following graphics show the market distribution in the last four years (See Table No. 1. Market Distribution 1992-1995).

Polifil is considered a reliable supplier, fully qualified to comply with customer requirements in terms of service, quality and innovation.

Polifil Industries, since March 1987, counts with an affiliate company in the United States named Pliana Inc. It is operated by Polifil Industries. Pliana is one of our major buyers in the United States and supplies the US market with yarn designated namely for the decoration market.[6] (See table No. 2. Pliana sales to customers in the USA in thousand pounds 1994 -1995).

From 1990 the aim of Polifil Industries was to concentrate its sales in the markets which proved to be more profitable. Therefore, rather than exporting to the variety of countries mentioned above, the export strategy focused in countries such as the United States (via Pliana Inc. as well as with direct shipments) and some countries in Central and South America as well as Australia.

The financial results of this strategy in regards to exports to the USA have been very satisfactory as the following graphic shows. (See table No. 3 and 4. Polifil Industries sales to the USA in US Dlls. 1992-1995).

Before NAFTA

In order to see the effects brought about by the implementation of the North American Free Trade Agreement, I will explain the prevailing situation in the following respects:

a) Import procedures:
- custom duties
- paper work

Polifil imports raw material such as polypropylene (resin), dispersions and lubricant preparations as well as spare parts for its machinery. These products are imported from the USA and have been imported since Polifil was created in the 1970's. 70% of Polifil imports are imported temporarily. Temporary imports do not pay taxes at all, they only pay the customs fee.

With respect to import duties, with NAFTA, they have diminished considerably. Duty fees vary according to the fraction. The rhythm of tax relief is as follows:

FRACTIONS CLASSIFIED AS	
A	immediate
B	5 years
C	10 years
B+	8 years
C+	6 years
X	not confirmed yet

For example, the resin which Polifil imports from the USA is a textile-fiber grade one and follows the bellow table:

YEAR	TAX TO PAY
1993	**10%**
1994	**8%**
1995	**8%**
1996	**7%**
1997	**6%**
1998	**5%**
1999	**4%**
2000	**3%**
2001	**0%**

If Polifil imports this resin from any other country, outside NAFTA, the tax would be 10%. With NAFTA, it saves 3%.

In the eight year period the total amount of taxes to be paid would be $635,690 US Dlls. The taxes not paid thanks to PITEX are $273,780 US Dlls. and the taxes not paid thanks to NAFTA are $72,380 US Dlls. The total amount of taxes to be paid is $289,530 US Dlls.

In regards to pigments, fraction 3206.49.02 paid 10% in 1993. Since NAFTA was implemented in 1994 pays 0%. This was one with an immediate tax deduction.

While fraction 3204.90.07 paid 5% in 1993. It will follow the below table:

YEAR	TAX TO PAY
1994	**4%**
1995	**3%**
1996	**2%**
1997	**1%**
1998	**0%**

NAFTA and PITEX will allow Polifil to save $106,973 US Dlls.

This represents substantial saving in terms of budget assigned for taxes. The percentage of the tax to pay has reduced considerably and in some cases there is no longer a tax to be paid. In 1994 Polifil saved about $65,790 U.S. Dlls. and in 1995 around $92,105.00 US Dlls.

Quotas have disappeared as well as import permits, this can be considered a benefit because these procedures used to be lengthy and hard to meet.

With respect to the paper work involved in import procedures, although it would appear that things have become easier for the importers, in fact they have become more bureaucratic.

Before GATT and NAFTA there were less requisites to fulfill. You only needed an import permit, to fall into the quota and to pay the tax. These were the tariff requisites. With GATT and NAFTA, tariff requisites disappeared, however non-tariff requisites have to be fulfilled and the certificate of origin became compulsory.

Although duties diminished and this is a substantial benefit as mentioned above, non-tariff barriers were created such as:

Letter of "Norma Oficial Mexicana (NOM)". Mexican Official Norm.
Labeling.
Technical Specifications.
Spreadsheet to determine customs value of imported goods according to the transaction method.
Certificate of origin.

During the administration of Carlos Salinas de Gortari many duties disappeared such as the ones pertaining to machinery and spare parts of the textile sector. From 1994, almost all types of textile machinery do not pay taxes. This has allowed textile factories to import new machinery tax free. However, the agreement does not make access to loans for machinery upgrading easier as it is only concerned with trade issues but not with financial matters.

Concerning import procedures Polifil experience has shown that with the treaty non-tariff requisites became more bureaucratic. This is considered a disadvantage. The benefits are manly tax relief, elimination of import quotas and elimination of import permits.

For the textile industry in general the benefits that have been obtained with NAFTA are mainly concerned with the reduction of duties. This allows textile factories to update their machinery importing it tax free. The spare parts of the machines also are tax free, so they save tax money when importing them.

b) Export Procedures:

- custom duties and export fractions.
- paper work.

With the Multi-fiber Agreement (MFA) the textile quota disappeared. Also the tax to be paid when importing textiles from Mexico in the USA. This had a psychological impact on the importers as they could buy more and cheaper (due to the devaluation) making their products remain competitive in the US market. As a result, sales to the USA have followed a growing trend.

Export Fractions

Product	Fraction	Tax relief
Chenille yarn.	5606	Immediate

5606 - Twisted yarn strips and similar forms of fractions 5404 or 5405 twisted (except the ones form fractions 5605 and the twisted mane yarn) chenille yarn, "chain stitch" yarn.

CONTINUOUS FIBER	5402.39	5 YEARS					
Year	1993	1994	1995	1996	1997	1998	1999
	10%	9%	7.20%	5.40%	3.60%	1.80%	0%

SHORT FIBER	5402.39	5 YEARS					
Year	1993	1994	1995	1996	1997	1998	1999
	10%	9%	7.20%	5.40%	3.60%	1.80%	0%

5402 - Synthetic filaments yarn (except sewing thread) not for retail sale.

CARPET	5702.42	10 YEARS					
Year	1993	1994	1995	1996	1997	1998	1999
	5.90%	5.30%	4.77%	4.24%	3.71%	3.18%	2.65%
	2000	2001	2002	2003	2004		
	2.12%	1.59%	1.06%	0.53%	0%		

Other fractions:

5509 - Discontinuous synthetic fiber yarn (except sewing thread) not for retail sale.
Discontinuous fiber (FICO - Short Fiber).
Fraction 5509.53 mixed exclusively or mainly with cotton.

(Table No. 5. Polifil Industries sales per product to the USA 1994 - 1995).

Before NAFTA there were a number of requisites to be fulfilled such as the quota and the export procedures related to the paper work involved which were too complicated and took long. With NAFTA quotas were eliminated and the number of documents were replaced by the Certificate of Origin.

Conclusions

To conclude, it can be said that Polifil is a good example of a successful textile industry that has been able to obtain a position in the international yarn market. This has been achieved through the years in part due to its ability to adjust to the logic of the market which is the logic of competitiveness and that the company has been benefited by NAFTA in the following respects:

Concerning import activities, tax relief, elimination of import quotas and elimination of import permits.

In its export activities, the elimination of quotas, the paper work involved reduced considerably and as a result time of response was optimized.

However, the case of Polifil is unique in nature and should not be applied to the textile industry in general. In fact, the performance of other textile industries has not been as optimistic as Polifil's.

In regards to the relative participation in the manufacture GNP, the textile sector has had a medium level participation and has had a falling trend.

In attention to the index of export specialization the textile sector has registered a low profile (lower than one). From 1983 onwards tended to especialize for the export market. However, the economic crisis of the eighties had an impact in this sector and it is until 1987 that we can talk about an important opening effect. Exports have continued to grow. Imports grew dramatically from 1988 onwards until the devaluation of 1994. Many industries have had to close their doors while the remaining ones have had to turn to the outside in search for new markets.

As I implied above, in an opening economy only the industries that have high levels of productivity, an adequate market strategy, technology, the right products and the most efficient distribution channels will be able to survive as this will allow them to compete in the international market under a free trade scheme.

Notes

1 Polypropylene is well established among the group of synthetic fibers, it has managed to be well accepted at world level regardless of the existence of other synthetic and artificial fibers which compete in the textile market.

2 ALTEX is the acronym of "Empresa Altamente Exportadora".

3 In 1974 Industrial Polifil was inaugurated. It was part of Group Pliana, which included Polifil Industries and later on, in 1987, Texel Industries as well. In September 1987, Group Pliana changed name to Texxel S.A de C.V. which in turn was part of Grupo Xabre. In July, 1992 Grupo Xabre sold Polifil and Texel. Texxel S.A. de C.V became the holding company.

4 Yarn such as chenille, textured, taslan which are used in decoration and fibers such as fico used for the production of tapestry and carpets as well as for the automotive industry.

5 In 1993, 54% of production was exported, in 1994 increased to 59% and in 1995 to 65%.

6 Other uses of polypropylene yarns are in the dressmaking industry of garments such as underwear, dressing gowns and nightgowns, pyjamas, socks, stockings and sports clothes like swimming suits, ballet leotards and tights as well as thermal clothes in general.

It is also used for manufacturing leisure and household items such as shawls, bedspreads, sleeping bag linings, tablecloths, shower curtains, kitchen gloves, shoes and sandals. Polypropylene products have also medical uses (i.e. surgical and sanitary) and in contrast with polyethylene, it can withstand heat sterilization temperatures without deformation.

Polypropylene sales have been growing rapidly for the last years. It has a wide range of desirable properties. This polymer has excellent processing, and it can be used to mold very thin wall parts.

Polypropylene is currently being used in Europe and in the United States for the manufacture of various types of clothes, due to the characteristics of the fiber, its easy care and hygiene as well as for its comfort properties.

Studies done by textile chemists, biologists, micro-biologists and engineers have brought to light all the advantages of this fiber that make it ideal for dressmaking for the following reasons:

1) Polypropylene is died before before converting it into fiber, that is, the coloring is added to the raw material previously to its extrusion. This makes the colour to be not only in the surface, but inside of the fiber, making impossible to decolour, as it happens in cotton, wool, polyester and nylon fibers, which are dyed after the fiber is raw. In this way, the colour remains only in the surface and it decolours easily at the exposure of agents such as sunlight, soaps and detergents, chemicals and normal wear.

2) The molecular constitution of polypropylene is very closed. The molecules are tightly linked and this avoids porosity in the fiber, causing that no liquid or solid material can penetrate it. As a result of this, stains remain in the surface, not inside. When cleaning or washing the stained cloth, the stain leaves and the cloth looks like brand new, it never wears not looses its colour.

Another advantage of its molecular structure is that when washed it dries very quickly, as water does not penetrate the fiber, but remains between the weave and the yarn.

It has been proved that polypropylene is highly hygienic in comparison with other fibers, it avoids the reproduction of bacteria, as it does not produce infections that are sometimes stimulated by the sweat of the skin in contact with clothes, nor allergies that are common in the use of other fibers.

4) Comfort is also an important point to mention. The humidity produced by the body slides through the polypropylene fibers and goes out to the exterior by evaporation in a fast way. This makes clothes to remain dry, avoiding the nuisances of skin marks of rubbing.

5) Polypropylene is the lightest fiber that exists in textiles, its specific weight is very low, therefore, polypropylene clothes are very light and comfortable.

6) Their resistance to chemical agents is very high, as they do not affect its texture nor colour and can be used without fear of wash or decolour of the cloth, some of them are: bleach, turpentine, thinner, gasoline and acetone.

7) Due to its constitution, polypropylene has great insulating and thermal properties. It has a very low heat conductivity, making clothes fresh in summer and warm in winter as they are easily molded to the atmosphere and body temperature.

8) Its resistance to wear and tear is higher to the one from other fibers, making its durability a lot more superior in time and use.

9) Its static electricity is very low, as a result of this it does not produce electricity shocks nor snaps when rubbed or in contact with skin and it does not stick to the body.

10) It does not held bad odors produced by sweat, as it does not absorb humidity.

11) It is easy to be taken care of. It can be washed at home and it does not require ironing.

12) Due to their resistance, clothes remain soft and nice to touch even after long use.

Clothes manufactured with polypropylene have the following advantages:

1) Firm colour
2) 100% washable, and stains are easily removed.
3) Hygienic and anti-allergenic.
4) They maintain the skin dry.
5) They are very light.
6) They are resistant to chemical agents.
7) They have thermal properties.
8) High resistance to wear.
9) Low static electricity.
10) They keep no odors.
11) Easy care
12) Soft and nice texture.

The textile industry is increasingly becoming one of "fashion plus price plus". The plus implies performance and value in addition to the usual aesthetics and cost that have earlier dominated the textile purchases. More and more consumers are expecting performance and quality in their textile purchases and polypropylene offers quality and good price.

Polypropylene is widely used by the automotive industry because of its high stiffness, scuff resistance and to the fact that it is not subject to environmental stress cracking and in general for its good processing characteristics.

Bibliography

Aguirre, Francisco G. **México en los Mercados Internacionales.** Grupo Imágenes de México. Edición Especial. No. 206. México, 1988.

Bergsten, C. Fred. **America in the World Economy. A strategy for the 1990's.** Institute for International Economics Washington D.C. 1988.

García Lourdes, Julio. **El Estado de Tlaxcala Hoy**. Libros de Oro y Guía de Exportadores. Grupo Auge. Edición Especial. Tomo X. Marzo, 1995.

Grinspun Ricardo and Maxwell A. Cameron. (eds.). **The Political Economy of North American Free Trade**. St. Martin's Press. New York, 1993.

El Economista (Mexico city newspaper).

El Financiero (Mexico city newspaper). Viernes 1 de Septiembre de 1995. Análisis Bolsa Mexicana de Valores. Mercado Bursátil p. 13A.

Jaime, Edna y Luis Barrón. **Lo hecho en México. Empresas mexicanas y apertura comercial**. Cal y Arena. México. 1992.

Siegert Lyle, Dorothy. **Performance of Textiles.** John Willey and Sons. USA. 1977.

Sittig, Marshall. **Polyolefin Production Processes. Latest Developments.** Chemical Technology Review No. 70. Noyes Data Corporation. Park Ridge, New Jersey, USA. 1976.

White, J. L. **Fiber Structure and Properties**. John Willey and Sons, Inc. (University of Tennessee) 1978.

ANNEXES

TABLE NO. 1
SOURCE: **POLIFIL STATISTICS**

TOTAL EXPORT SALES OF POLIFIL INDUSTRIES IN 1993

COUNTRY	PERCENTAGE
USA	83.3
AUSTRALIA	9.5
VENEZUELA	3.2
GUATEMALA	2.1
ECUADOR	1.7
EUROPEAN UNION	0.18

(See Graphic No. 1)

TOTAL EXPORT SALES OF POLIFIL INDUSTRIES IN 1994

COUNTRY	PERCENTAGE
USA	88
AUSTRALIA	9.5
GUATEMALA	1.2
VENEZUELA	0.7
EUROPEAN UNION	0.6

(See Graphic No. 2)

TOTAL EXPORT SALES OF POLIFIL INDUSTRIES IN 1995

COUNTRY	PERCENTAGE
USA	90
VENEZUELA	5.5
AUSTRALIA	2.8
GUATEMALA	0.7
INDONESIA	0.7
EUROPEAN UNION	0.3

(See Graphic No. 3)

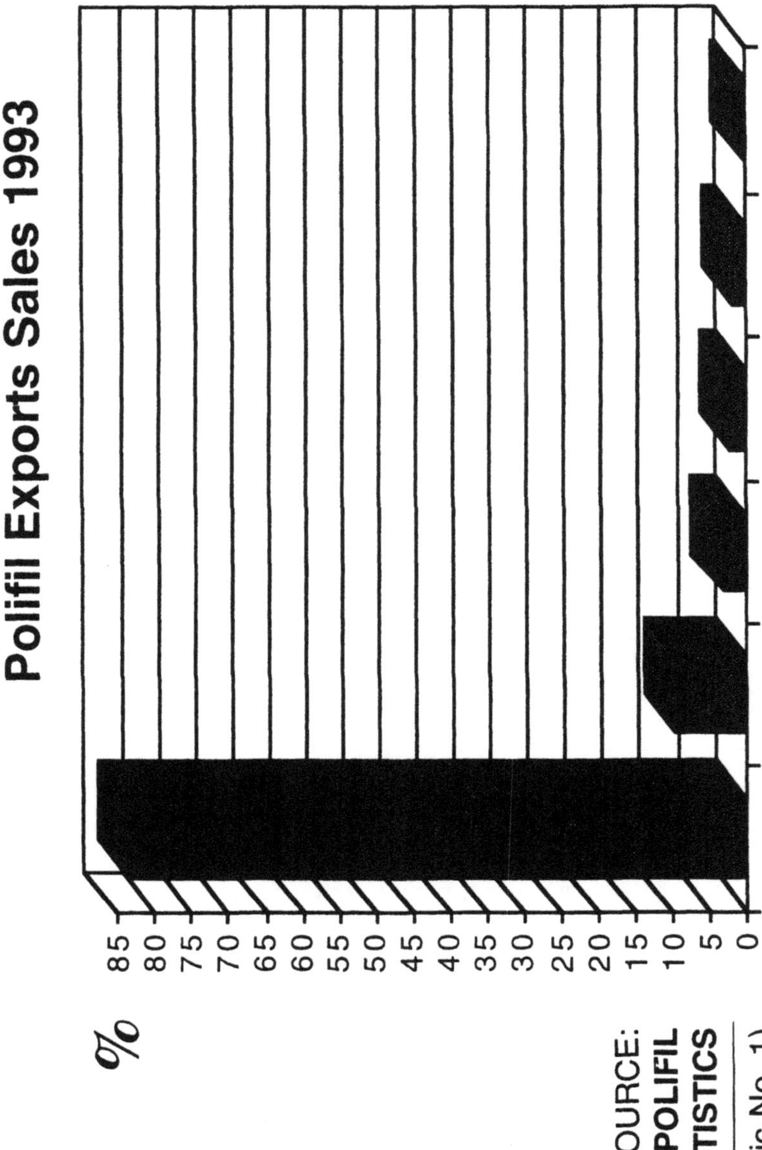

SOURCE: **POLIFIL STATISTICS**

(Graphic No. 1)

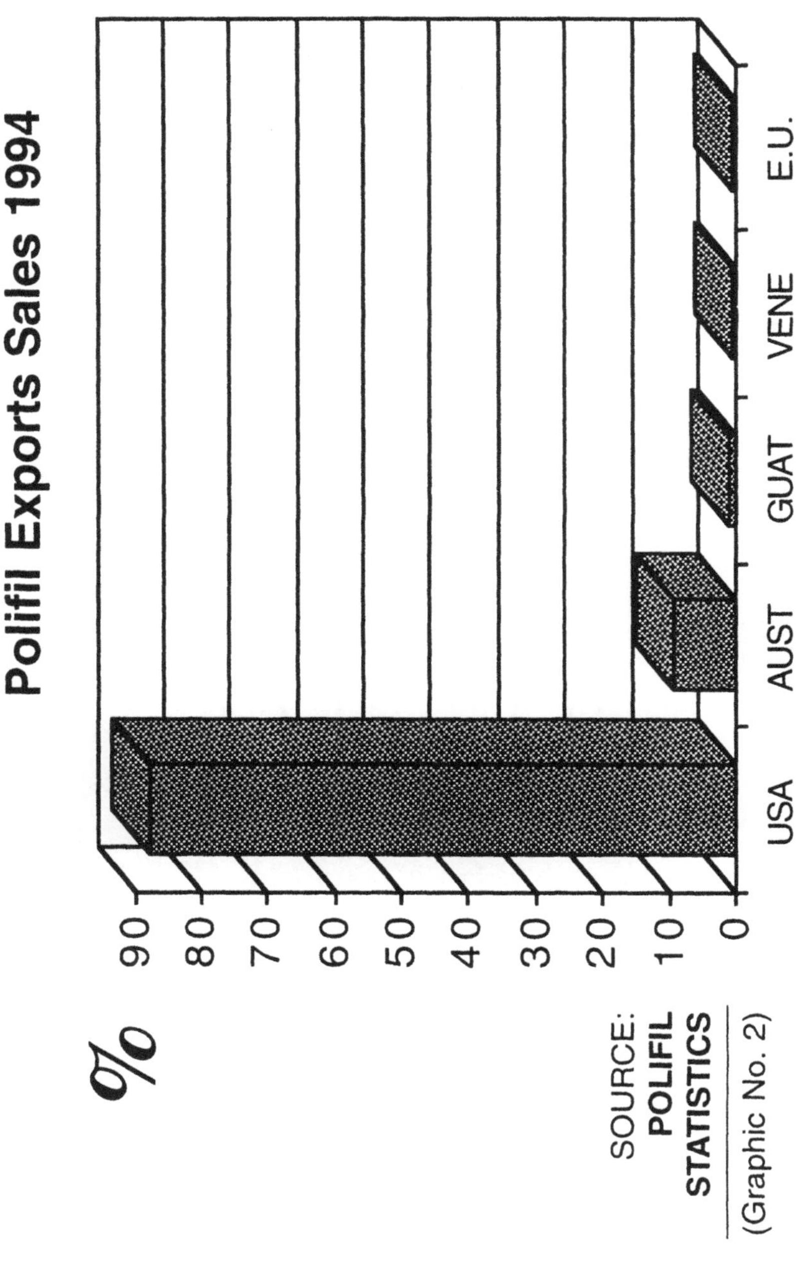
Polifil Exports Sales 1994
%
90
80
70
60
50
40
30
20
10
0
USA
AUST
GUAT
VENE
E.U.
SOURCE:
POLIFIL
STATISTICS
(Graphic No. 2)

Polifil Exports Sales 1995

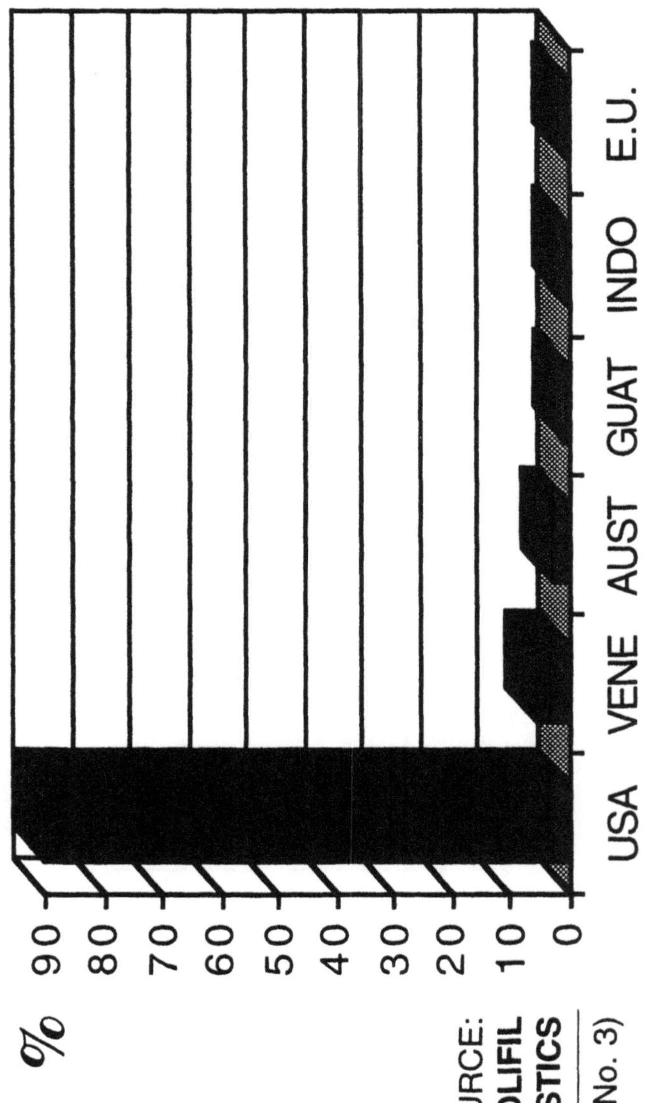

SOURCE: **POLIFIL STATISTICS**

(Graphic No. 3)

TABLE NO. 2
SOURCE: **POLIFIL STATISTICS**

PLIANA INC. SALES TO CUSTOMERS IN THE U.S.A.
IN THOUSAND POUNDS 1994-1995

1994	1995
6,386	7,139

(See Graphic No. 4)

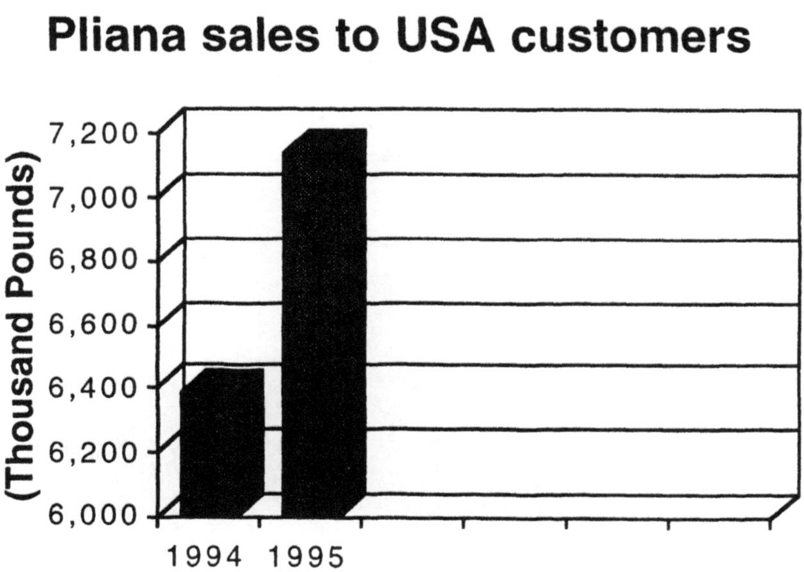

SOURCE:
POLIFIL
STATISTICS

(Graphic No. 4)

TABLE NO. 3
SOURCE: **POLIFIL STATISTICS**

POLIFIL INDUSTRIES SALES TO THE U.S.A.
IN U.S. DLLS. 1992-1995

YEAR	U.S. DLLS.
1992	8,383,712
1993	13,738,623
1994	18,845,510
1995	20,620,056

(See Graphic No. 5)

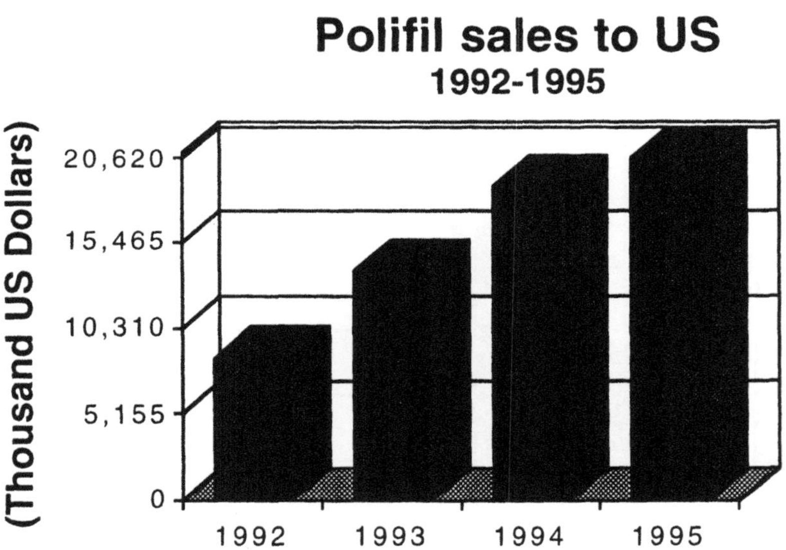

SOURCE:
POLIFIL
STATISTICS

(Graphic No. 5)

TABLE NO. 4
SOURCE: **POLIFIL STATISTICS**

**POLIFIL INDUSTRIES SALES TO THE U.S.A.
IN KGS. 1992-1995**

YEAR	KGS.
1992	2,116,668
1993	3,138,774
1994	3,976,087
1995	4,209,992

**POLIFIL INDUSTRIES SALES TO THE U.S.A.
IN METRIC TONS 1992-1995**

YEAR	TONS
1992	2,117
1993	3,139
1994	3,976
1995	4,210

(See Graphic No. 6)

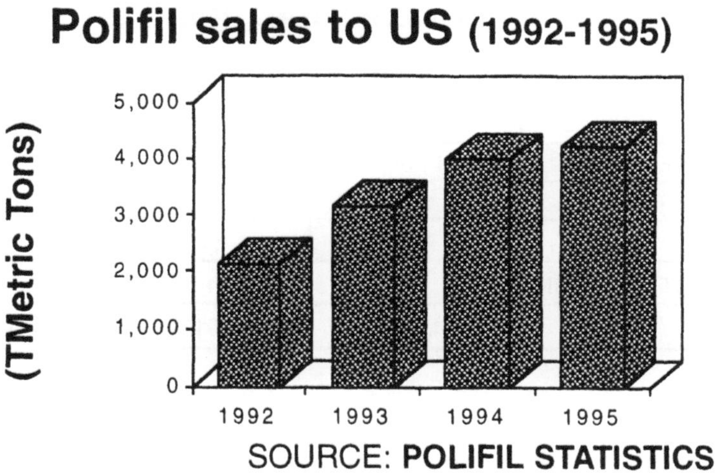

(Graphic No. 6)

TABLE NO. 5
SOURCE: **POLIFIL STATISTICS**

POLIFIL INDUSTRIES SALES PER PRODUCT TO THE U.S.A. IN METRIC TONS. 1994

PRODUCT	PLIANA	JOAN FRABRICS	ROSSVILLE
CHENILLE	1,104	517	111
TEXTURED	1,287	653	30
TASLAN	35	8	0
FICO	193	0.15	0
TOTAL	2,619	1,178	141

(See Graphic No. 7)

POLIFIL INDUSTRIES SALES PER PRODUCT TO THE U.S.A. IN METRIC TONS. 1995

PRODUCT	PLIANA	JOAN FRABRICS	ROSSVILLE
CHENILLE	896	213	642
TEXTURED	1,256	736	218
TASLAN	129	51	0
FICO	76	12	0
COTTON YARN	0	1	0
TOTAL	2,357	1,013	860

(See Graphic No. 8)

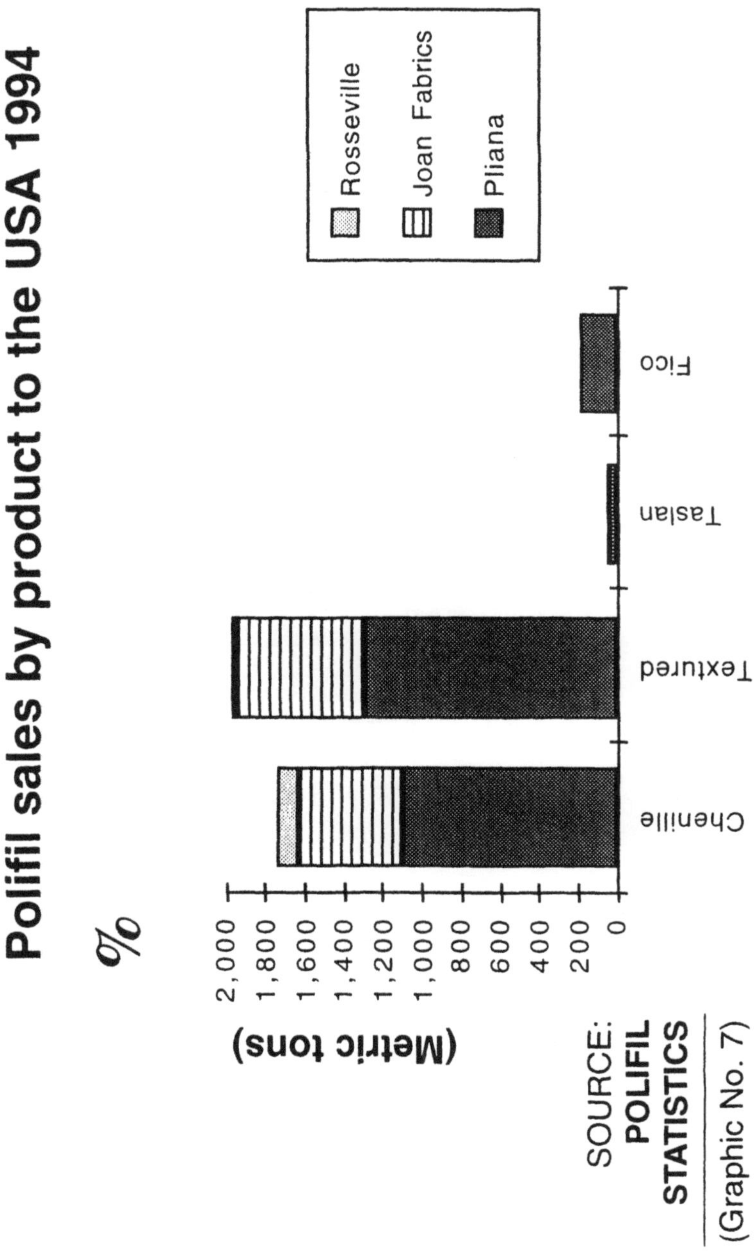
Polifil sales by product to the USA 1994
%
(Metric tons)
2,000
1,800
1,600
1,400
1,200
1,000
800
600
400
200
0
Chenille
Textured
Taslan
Fico
Rosseville
Joan Fabrics
Pliana
SOURCE: POLIFIL STATISTICS
(Graphic No. 7)

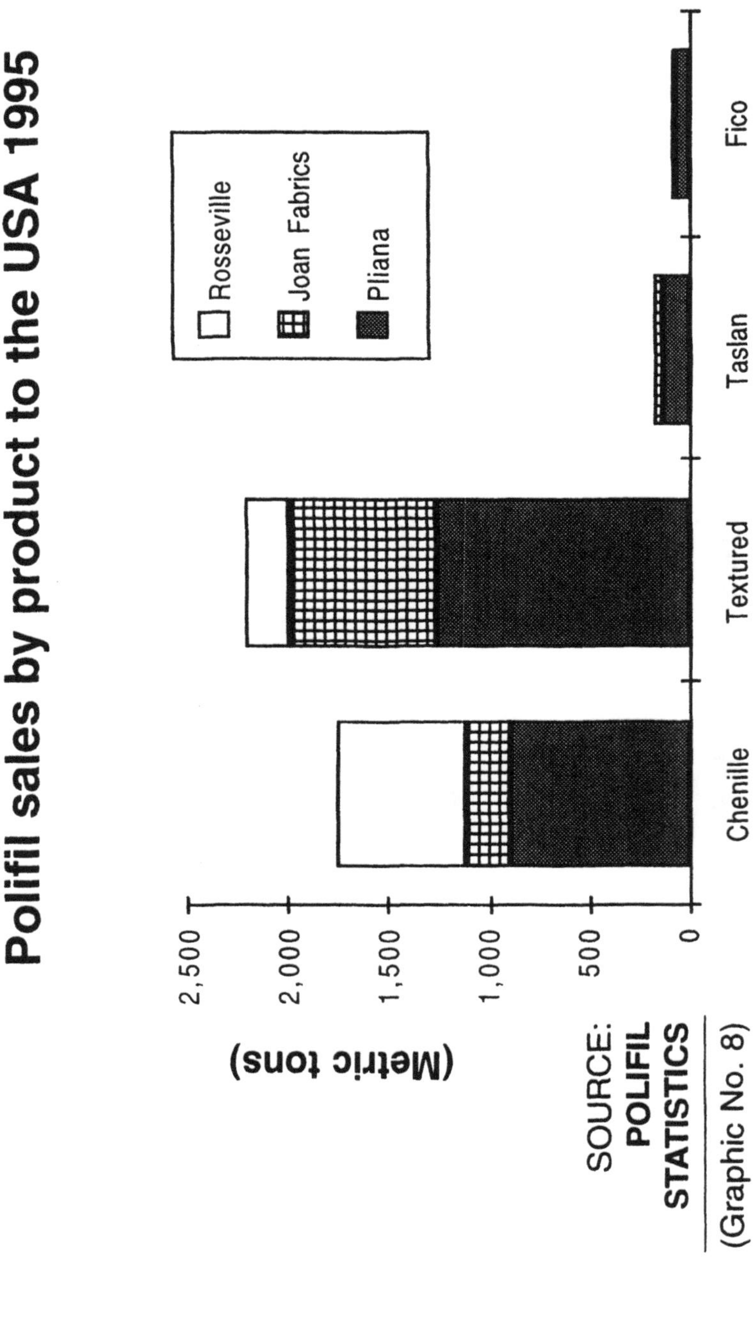
Polifil sales by product to the USA 1995
(Metric tons)
2,500
2,000
1,500
1,000
500
0
Rosseville
Joan Fabrics
Pliana
Chenille
Textured
Taslan
Fico
SOURCE: POLIFIL STATISTICS
(Graphic No. 8)

Part II

Chapter IV

Academic Issues in Canada Arising From NAFTA

Guy Claveau

I would like to present an overview of the academic issues that arose following the signing of the North American Free Trade Agreement. The list does not include the publications of the last three months since the data banks consulted are updated only every three months. The questions asked are as follows: do they refer to the orientation of the research, to the establishment of infrastructures to facilitate integration or to raise interest in the development of a continental identity called the North American Union?

Research orientation?

It is interesting to note that the latest studies on NAFTA by researchers in Canada were carried out as a result of an internal political agenda. Indeed, last October 30, the Quebec referendum on sovereignty presented a serious problem to researchers in the various social science disciplines. Faced with the possibility of Quebec becoming an independent state, could it be assumed that the new country would automatically join the group or should the negotiation process of the treaty be reopened?

According to Ivan Bernier, a Laval University legal scholar, the

the matter and a purely political viewpoint. Accession of the new country to NAFTA would not come automatically (La Presse, September 1995).

The second opinion on the legal interpretation of Section 2204, para. 2 on accession, developed by Loungnarath, Vilaysoun of the Faculty of Law of the University of Montreal, is that "Quebec cannot be blocked by a partner in the exporting of its goods and services to other partners" (the American law firm of Rogers and Wells, 1995). It is a question of negotiating the conditions of accession not renegotiating accession itself. In the context of GATT or of the various widenings of the European Community, negotiations on the accession of a country usually dealt with how to adapt the institutional mechanisms and other transitional measures. The series of studies ordered by the Quebec government of l'Institut National de la Recherche Scientifique (INRS) (National Institute of Scientific Research) of the University of Quebec at a cost of tens of millions of dollars will not soon be forgotten.

Still in the area of politics, the studies (Charles Doran and Gregory Marchildon, 1995) revealed other findings. In all three countries, the parties in power when the agreements were signed had changed their positions. The Conservatives under Brian Mulroney, who were against free trade in 1984, had by the 90s developed a business approach which gave them a solid electoral footing in Quebec and in the West against Ontario which opposed the Agreement. The well-known position of the Republicans in the U.S. changed when the unions objected to the transfer of industrial production to countries with low salary levels. The goal of a single trading area from Alaska to Tierra del Fuego now belongs to Bill Clinton's Democrats. Finally, there is really no point in bringing up here the evolution of the PRI.

A glance at dissertation abstracts for the last two years shows that ten documents have been presented. The following are the topics related to NAFTA: banking services, the Canadian perspective, agreements on government procurement, the need for a dispute settlement mechanism for Havana and other areas, the environment as dealt with in Chapter 9 of the treaty, the loss of women's jobs, sustainable development, the regulation of foreign investment in Mexico, and NAFTA and the Commonwealth of English-speaking countries of the Caribbean and Latin America.

Research on Canadian economic viewpoints (R. Wonnacott; Ann Weston, 1995) reveals that the "Canadian government has been successful in gaining access to a rapidly growing Mexican market on terms as favourable as those of the United States". Wonnacott thinks that with tariff-free access to inexpensive supplies of intermediate goods produced in Mexico, NAFTA is superior to treaties like GATT which allow developing countries to maintain their own barriers against free imports. For Ann Weston, Canadians evaluate NAFTA "through the lens of the Canadian experience under the CUSFTA" and the latter agreement "has not been altogether rosy" and "was probably oversold". The day that NAFTA came into effect the public was shocked by the way the Mexican army crushed an uprising in the State of Chiapas. Reactions for and against the Agreement were expressed. The studies of the North-South Institute revealed that both opinions were at fault. "Regional integration brings with it new interests and responsibilities for the internal affairs of each other's country." The side agreements on the environment and labour show this clearly. Furthermore, this prestigious Institute suggested asymmetrical liberalization, i.e. Canada and the U.S. liberalizing imports more rapidly to facilitate broader social policy initiatives thus increasing the number of people able to take advantage of the situation (North-South, 1994).

A survey of Microlog, a Canadian research index of all levels of government (particularly federal and provincial) showed 156 references to NAFTA over the last three years. Most are specific market studies of various economic sectors such as fisheries, plastics, tourism, construction, the environment, biodiversity, oil, mineral investment capital or the processes involved in accessing the Mexican market in both the public and private sectors. Public organizations financed studies based on the need for information; the following are the topics involved: archaeology and national parks, weather and transportation, language planning and the canyon wren.

¿Infrastructure?

Although Team Canada did not visit Mexico as part of the promotion of globalization, a number of activities were undertaken by departments and agencies of the government of Canada and their counterparts in Mexico following the signing of NAFTA. Research trends in these various sectors show a gradual movement away from the "simple provision of finance for promotion of industrial activity toward a role that emphasizes the need to create and maintain sources of market intelligence and to generate market strategies" (Mullin, 1995). The International Trade Business Plan (subtitled "An Integrated Plan for Trade Investment and Technology Promotion and Development") and Prospectus Mexico-Canada: Partnering for Success are two publications aimed at managers interested in the

Mexican market. The "Access North Americas" program, which links Mexican needs with Canadian strengths, provided a funding of $27 million between 1993 and 1996. Other resources are available to further exploratory studies in such fields as biotechnology, telecommunications (distance learning), the environment, forestry, agriculture, geomatics, etc.

With an aggregate budget of almost $10 million, CIDA and IDRC by means of interagency cooperation try to promote cooperation between Canadian universities and Mexican partners in research and academic activities. What was the content of the government's position at Wingspread? In 1992, participants from the three countries agreed that:

• internationalization of the third level of education is the key to a better quality and a higher standard of living as well as to a better understanding of distinctive cultures and identities;

• education is a component of stronger partnerships.

To achieve those objectives there must be access to the vast North American potential and effective development of trilateral collaboration as a support for bilateral relations with third countries and international organizations. The means suggested in this regard were:

• development of a North American dimension in higher education;

• sharing information on issues of common concern and on experiences of common interest;

• promotion of student and faculty mobility; and

• promotion of collaboration among educational institutions, public authorities and business exploitation of the full potential of information management and transmission technologies.

In support of those objectives and to monitor the framework agreement, the Vancouver Symposium established a trilateral task force which began taking inventory. The findings were presented at a second event called the Symposium of Vancouver 1993. The survey of ANUIES involved 77 associate universities of which 30 reported agreements with counterparts in the United States and Canada, 193 with the former and 22 with the latter. Social sciences and management topped the list with the United States while engineering was first for links with Canada. The AUCC data base indicates that, among 89 Canadian member universities, 36 are engaged in a total of 101 agreements (68 with the U.S. and 33 with Mexico).

The Institute of International Education (IIE), with a mandate from the Office of Academic Programs, did a survey of 3,444 accredited colleges and universities and found 182 linkages with Mexican counterparts and 109 with Canada. The 1994 survey shows that 199

U.S. students went to Canada on institutional linkage programs, while 1,194 went to Mexico on the same programs.

Political involvement following the process of integration was shown by an investment of $10 million in three years (1995, 96 and 97) in the Program for North American Mobility, a cooperative partnership involving the governments of Canada, Mexico and the United States. The program is designed to support joint projects among universities.

Human Resources Development Canada announced the participation of 200 Canadian students a year in training and internship. At the provincial level, the Conference of Rectors of Quebec signed a number of student exchanges in 1995. The Government of Ontario (OCGS) is negotiating with the National Council on Science and Technology (CONOCIT) for a 1996 agreement that will provide access to graduate schools to up to 100 Mexican graduate students each year.

Another event in the area of the institutionalization of educational exchanges is certainly the establishment of the Université Nationale Autonome de Mexico (UNAM) (Autonomous National University of Mexico) in Hull in the National Capital area. Courses in the Spanish language, in Mexican civilization and history, and the history of Mexican art and literature will provide a better understanding of the third partner.

More specifically focused seminars such as the one organized in 1995 by McGill and the Instituto Latinoamericano de Estudios Transnacionales in Mexico on the problems of boundaries and culture illustrate present research on the understanding of cultural diversity.

North American Identity

According to Bruce Campbell, "It is a fiction that Nafta is a free trade agreement. While admittedly this language made the Agreement easier to sell, it hides the true magnitude of what Canada is a part of" (Bruce Campbell, 1995). In reality, the process of integration covers financial services, transportation, telecommunication, a policy on the environment, and all social and economic dimensions. It establishes continental regimes, rules and procedures for harmonization standards in a number of areas such as professional qualifications, food inspection, health, etc. This was well understood by the politician who, testifying before the House of Commons, stated: "The pressure to bring our laws and customs into line with those of the dominant partner would be continuous... leading to a progressive erosion of Canadian independence and identity" (Bruce Campbell, 1995).

The debates about the Free Trade Agreement (FTA) between Canada and the United States and the North American Free Trade Agreement (NAFTA) involving all three North American countries were very different in Quebec compared to English Canada. Many prominent members of the art and literature community opposed free trade for fear that it would weaken Canadian national identity; because the national identity this community sought to protect was clearly English, the argument encouraged many in Quebec to favour the agreements. A major group of trade unionists from Quebec who opposed NAFTA did not oppose free trade, as did unions in English Canada (Peter Bakvis, 1995).

Research on the matter of identity is still ongoing. As Joseph Duffey, Director of the United States Information Agency, stressed at the 1993 Vancouver symposium, breaking down trade barriers is not enough to ensure economic success. He suggests that more attention should be given to developing a sense of a North American identity. In this regard, the commitment of educational institutions and the acknowledgement of cultural dimensions and differences are only the beginning of the process.

References

Affaires étrangères et commerce international Canada, **Budget des dépenses 1995-1996,** Ottawa, Gouvernement du Canada, 1995. 150p.

Bakvis Peter, **Free Trade in North America: Divergent Perspectives between Quebec and English.** Journal citation: Québec Studies, 1993, 16:39-48.

Campbell Bruce, in **Canadian Foreign Policy, Trade and Investment Policy under NAFTA: as if Jobs Matteered.** Ottawa, Carleton University, Spring 1994. 195p.

Doran Charles, Marchildon Gregory, **The Nafta Puzzle, Political Parties and trade in North America,** Boulder, Colo., Westview Press. 1995, 264p.

Institut Nord-Sud, **Question-clés pour la politique étrangère canadienne**, Ottawa, Institut Nord-Sud, 1994. 62p.

Mullin James, Breaking through together, **Focal, Canadian Foundation for the Americas,** 1995. 30p.

North American Higher Education Cooperation, New York, Institute of International Education, 1993. 112p.

North American Higher Education Cooperation, **Report on the International Symposium on Higher Education and Strategic Partnerships Vancouver, September 10-13, 1993,** Worldstat International Inc, 1993. 111p.

Nafta as a Model of Development: the Benefits and Cost of Merging High- and Low-Wage Areas. New York, Ed. Richard S. Belous and Jonathan Lemco, State University of New York Press, 1995. 216p.

Proceedings of the Roundtable Conference on Trilateralizing Business Education, Texas, ed. S. Kerry Cooper & Julian E. Gaspar, 1993. 140p.

Serfaty, Meir. The Promotion of Canadian Universities in Mexico, Argentina and Chili, Ottawa, AUCC, 1994. 58p.

Twaites James, **Le libre-échange et le milieu des affaires**, Cité libre, 22, no.5, sept-oct. 1994, p. 14-23.

Electronic Resources on CD-ROMS

ABC Political Science Ondisc (1994 -)
Actualité Québec (1990-)
America History and Life1987-)
Canadian Bussines and Current Affairs (1982-)
Dissertation Abstracts Ondisc(1861-)
Francis (1994 -)
Historical Abstracts (1982-)
Microlog: Canadian Reserch Index/Index de Recherche Du Canada
Repère (1980-)

Chapter V

North American Free Trade Agreement: Evaluation on Cultural Sector

Michelle Bussières

Trade Obligation with Regard to Cultural Industries

Free Trade Agreement between the United States and Canada (FTA)

Article 2005: Cultural Industries

1. Cultural industries are exempt from the provisions of this Agreement, except as specifically provided in Article 401 (Tariff Elimination), paragraph 4 of Article 1607 (divestiture of an indirect acquisition) and Articles 2006 and 2007 of this Chapter.

2. Notwithstanding any other provision of this Agreement, a Party may take measures of equivalent commercial effect in response to actions that would have been inconsistent with this Agreement but for paragraph 1.

Article 2012: Definitions

For purposes of this Chapter: cultural industry means an enterprise engaged in any of the following activities:

a) the publication, distribution, or sale of books, magazines, periodicals, or newspaper in print or machine readable form but not including the sole activity of printing or typesetting any of the foregoing,

b) the production, distribution, sale or exhibition of film or video recordings,

c) the production, distribution, sale or exhibition of audio or video music recordings,

d) the publication, distribution, or sale of music in print or machine readable form, or

e) radio communication in wich the transmissions are intended for direct reception by general public, and all radio, television and cable television broadcasting undertakings and all satellite programming and broadcast network services.

From the beginning of the negotiations, Canadians expressed concern that an agreement might erode the government's capacity to encourage and help Canada's cultural industries (film and video , music and sound recording, publishing, cable transmission and broadcasting) and thus to contribute to the development of Canada's unique cultural identity.[1]

In order to remove any ambiguity that Canada's unique cultural identity remains untouched by the four very limited exceptions, nothing in this agreement affects the ability of either Party to pursue cultural policies.

The specific exceptions are:

• the elimination of tariffs on any inputs to, and products of, the cultural industries, such as musical instruments, cassettes, film, recording tape, records cameras (Article 401);

• any requirement to sell a foreign-owned enterprise engaged in a cultural activity acquired indirectly through the purchase of its parent will be balanced by an offer to purchase the enterprise at fair open market value (paragraph 4 of Article 1607);

• both parties will provide copyright protection to owners of programs broadcast by distant stations and retransmitted by cable companies; this undertaking will be on a non-discriminatory basis; after Canadian legislation is implemented there will be an opportunity for further review of outstanding issues in both countries (Article 2006);

• the requirement that a magazine or newspaper must be typeset and printed in Canada in order for advertisers to be able to deduct their expenses for advertising space in that magazine will be eliminated(Article 2007).

• Canadian position was tempered by inclusion of Article 2005, paragraph 2, which constrains the two Parties to give proof of cautionousness with regards to trade incidences of measures put in place.

North American Free Trade Agreement between the United States, Mexicoo and Canada (NAFTA)

The exclusion of the cultural sector from the FTA was extended in the NAFTA but only for trade between Canada and United States, and Canada and Mexico.

Annex 2106: Cultural Industries

Notwithstanding any other provision of this Agreement, as between Canada and the United States, any measure adopted or maintained with respect to cultural industries, excepy as specifically provided in Article 302 (Market Access-Tariff Elimination), and any measure of equivalent commercial effect taken in response, shall be governed under this Agreement exclusively in accordance with the provisions of the Canada-United States Free Trade Agreement. The rights and obligations between Canada and any other Party with respect to such measures shall be identical to those applying between Canada and the United States.

Article 2107: Definitions

For purposes of this Chapter:

cultural industries means persons engaged in any of the following activities:

a) the publication, distribution, or sale of books, magazines, periodicals or newspapers in print or machine readable form but not including the sole activity of printing or typesetting any of the foregoing;

b) the production, distribution, sale or exhibition of film or video recordings;

c) the production, distribution, sale or exhibition of audio or video music recordings;

d) the publication, distribution or sale of music in print or machine readable form; or

e) radiocommunications in which the transmissions are intended for direct reception by the general public, and all radio, television and cable broadcasting undertakings and all satellite programming and broadcast network services.

NAFTA makes provision for exceptions as regards cultural industries, national security, taxation, the balance of payments and areas mentioned in Article XX of GATT, dealing with general exceptions.

Québec has always deemed cultural industries to be important. Article 2106 excludes them from the scope of NAFTA. The article stipulates that the rights and obligations respecting cultural industries contemplated in the FTA between in Canada and the United States will automatically apply to Canada and Mexico, or between Canada and any other nation that joins the free trade area.

Article 2005 of the FTA also exempts cultural industtries from all the FTA's provisions except those pertaining to the gradual elimination of customs duties, e.g. duties on musical instruments, records, magnetic tapes and cameras. Any signatory country is authorized to take measures with an equivalent commercial effect in response to intervention by another country in the free trade area that is incompatible with the FTA or NAFTA.

From a Québec standpoint, NAFTA adequately protects cultural industries. During the trilateral negotiations, the government insisted that exclusion in the FTA also be incorporated into NAFTA.

However, the US Trade Act, and the North American Fre Trade Agreement Implementation Act (103rd Congress, 1st Session) approved by President on December 8th, 1993, authorize the American government to identify countries which do not give adequate access to American interests and then, to ask an inquiry under Section 301.

World Trade Organization / GATT of 1994

The agreement on WTO includes an agreement on services. The approach to liberalization in the GATS (General Agreement on Trade and Services) is different from the one in NAFTA. Where in NAFTA all services are liberalized except sector specifically identified, the approach in GATS is that only service sectors identified by parties in their list of commitments are liberalized.

Canadian position during the multilateral negociations

During the negociation Canada favoured a general exception for cultural industries in the GATS. This was supported, but only late in the negociation by France.

Because of the opposition mainly from the United States, a general exception could not be agreed upon.

To achieve the same level of protection for its cultural industries as the one in NAFTA, Canada took no commitments in the cultural sector in GATS. The E.U. did the same despite the strong opposition from the Americans supported by their movies industry.

Trade in Cultural Industries

Consistently during international trade negociations, Canada has always wanted to maintain protection to its cultural industries.

This position is obviously motivated by the strenght and the proximity of the U.S. cultural industries and the fact that 75% of Canada share common language with the Americans.

Despite all the structural protection to its cultural industries, Canada remains an open market to foreign cultural products.

Statistics on cultural products in Canada are indicative of this openess:

- 60% of the books
- 90% of the records
- 64% of television programs
- 94% of films

are produced abroad, overwhelingly in the U.S.

In Québec those numbers would be far less important, especially for books and television programs, through the languaje specifity and "distinct society".- Eventhough cultural industries are excluded from the trade rules, this did not preclude the development of trade disputes between U.S. and Canada in recent months.

Trade disputes case between tue United States and Canada

Country Music Television

In June 1994, the Canadian Radio-Television and Telecommunications Commission (CRTC) decided to withdraw a broadcast license from a U.S. owned cable television service, Country Music Television (CMT), to broadcast its programs in Canada and gave it to a canadian-owned country music channel.

CMT filed a Section 301 petition with the Office of the U.S. Trade Representative (USTR) December 23, 1994, estimating its losses from the Canadian action to beat at least $63 million US.

Canadian Trade Minister, Roy MacLaren, said that the Canadian government has no power to overturn the decision by Canadian regulators. The CRTC decision was upheld by Canadian court in December 1994.

Canadian officials argued that the action by the CRTC did not constitute a violation of NAFTA, because the issue of services in cultural industries is effectively exempted from that agreement.

CMT argued that the Canadian action violates the investment and national treatment for services provisions of the NAFTA, and that the cultural exemptions cannot be invoked to justify the action.

In June 1995, the U.S. dropped its plan to publish a trade sanctions list against Canada on denying license applications through the U.S. Federal Communications Commission for Canadian-owned services to operate in the U.S. in a fight over access for U.S. broadcasters after (CMT and the New Country Network (Canadian Company) reached a commercial agreement in which the U.S. owned CMT will acquire a minority share of its Canadian rival. The merger has been approved by the CRTC.

According to USTR, the commercial deal did not address the broader question of Canada's policy of removing foreign-owned channels if Canadian regulators determine that there is a directly competitive Canadian-owned operation.

Taxes on Split-run edition of U.S. magazines

On December 22nd, 1994, Canadian Heritage Minister, Michel Dupuy, announced an excise tax on advertising revenues generated in Canada by certains editions of U.S. magazines sold in Canada.

The U.S. magazine industry alleged that the expected 80 percent excise tax on advertising in Canadian editions of U.S. magazines shipped electronically - in particular, Sports Illustrated - would block their access to the Canadian market.

The Office of the U.S. Trade Representative threatened retaliation, saving that the proposal was intended to prevent publication of Sports Illustrated Canada, despite its strong readership.

On June 19th, 1995, the Canadian government announced it would impose a new excise tax on advertising in Canadian split-run edition of foreign magazines. An anti-avoidance rule would also be added to the Income Tax Act to prevent the deductibility of advertising expenses in non-Canadian newspapers and periodicals.

The changes to the Excise Tax Act would impose a levy equivalent to 80 percent of the value of all advertisements carried in a Canadian split-run edition. A split-run edition would be defined as one that is distributed in Canada, that contains more than 20 percent editorial material not original to the Canadian market, and that contains one or more advertisements directed at Canadians.

The Canadian proposed law should be adopted by the end of the year.

Sports Illustrated considers challenging the law in front of Canadian courts.

Audiotapes Taxes

On December 22nd, 1995, Canadian Heritage Minister, Michel Dupuy, announced that Canada would impose a levy (0,25 cents CAN) on blank audiotapes funds for Canadian recording artist and music producers to compesate them for revenue lost as a result of home recording and piracy.

American record industry argued that American owners of copyrightt will not be compensated by the Canadian funds.

Canadian Films Barriers Listed

The Motion Picture (MPA) has published its annual list of foreign country barriers to U.S. filmed and video entertaiment products. Allegations against Québec's Cinema Act are highlighted in the report, although the MPA levels its sharpest attacks against markets in the Far East Europe.

In the chapter on Canada the MPA details a list of trade barriers that U.S. film, television program, and home video producers and distributors alleged to face. There are complaints about quantitative restrictions, such as broadcast quotas regulating the annual share of non-Canadian pogramming and budget resources, as well as other broadcasting regulations and policies that restrict the carriage of U.S. signals and services.

With particular regard to Québec, the MPA considers the Québec Cinema Act a high-priority trade barrier:

The Québec Act stipulates that in order to distribute videos in Québec, it is necessary to obtain a License from the Régie du Cinéma. Only Québec-based companies are eligible for such licenses, except on a title-by-title basis, if a non-Québec distributor can prove that it is either the producer or the holder of worlwide rights.

These restrictives practices imposing higher cost are seen by the MPA as a serious impediments to the full development of the Québec market.

Conclusion

Recent developments have shown that the opening of border to trade in goods as well as in services, on a global or regional basis, will accelerate in future.

This liberalization is accompanied by an intensification in the movement of people which creates favourable conditions for more cultural exchanges.

The growth in trade of services exceeds trade in goods. Big economic interests are often at stake in the opening of markets to cultural products. As example Hollywood is among the biggest U.S. exporters.

At the same time, development of the technology opens new ways to spread cultural products across borders. One has only to think of broadcast by satellite or of internet to imagine the breaking of traditional limits to the exchange of cultural products.

Because of that, the governments will face more pressure from their domestic industries to put in place protection while at the same time they will have to face pressure from their trading partners and from technological developments to open borders.

Already some members of the U.S. Congress, in discussions surrounding the granting of "fast track authority" to the Administration for trade negociations, have expressed their view that no "cultural exception" should be agreed upon in new trade agreements.

Based like the one given to Canada on that it is safe to say that both, trade libralization for cultural industries, and trade protection for cultural industries, will be a top priority in future trade negociations.

Chapter VI

Higher Education, NAFTA and Canadian Foreign Policy: Three Themes in Search of Convergence

Meir Serfaty

Introduction

1995 witnessed the successful culmination of numerous efforts by the academic and related communities to include cultural and educational affairs within the framework of Canada's foreign policy. Simultaneously and as an expression of Canada's desire to expand its educational activities with the U.S. and Mexico, a number of initiatives was officially undertaken by the Canadian government in collaboration with independent educational organisms. These initiatives were designed to bring the educational component of foreign policy into sharper focus and to integrate it more fully into the foreign policy agenda.

This paper discusses a few of the more significant developments in relation to NAFTA's second year of existence from the Canadian perspective and in the realm of higher education.[1] It makes no attempt to be descriptive or comprehensive in its treatment of the subject (for example, by drawing on specific examples of collaboration). Rather, it endeavours to offer an analysis of the manner in which culture and post-secondary education became a new pillar of Canada's foreign policy in 1995. As befits the parameters of this forum, the focus is on the ramification of this change on events of 1995 and on NAFTA perspectives. It is this writer's view, however, that understanding the context of current initiatives will prove instructive to the participants of this forum.

Briefly stated, the paper is predicated on assertions made elsewhere that Canadian foreign policy is both statist and obsessed with international trade. It argues that once Canadian education adopted a model of globalization based primarily on economic considerations, the state had little difficulty incorporating it as a pillar of its foreign policy. By its very nature, NAFTA may become an ideal mutually beneficial vehicle for the perceived needs of both the federal governments and the universities; but as evidenced by events in 1995, Canadian higher education appears to continue to march to the tune of the federal drummer.

The Antecedents of Convergence

It is evident that, aside from its importance in overseas development assistance projects, academic concerns did not fare well in the past as tools of Canadian foreign policy. As recently as 1993, an informed observer of Canada's role in the world failed to make even a passing reference to their significance,[2] whether actual or possible in the context of traditional Canadian multilateral thrusts abroad. Two post-war foreign policy reviews, conducted in 1969-70 and 1985-86, emphasized detente, unity and independence, and international security and competitiveness, independence and internationalization, respectively, as objectives worth seeking. Essentially, these translated themselves into a search for collective security (primarily through its role in peace-keeping) and, especially in the 1980s and 1990s, international trade. Developmental aid and enhancement of human rights appeared to be useful appendices to these policy objectives. Similarly, the propagation of Canadian culture and education abroad was pursued by autonomous organizations such as the IACS, CBIE, as well as universities and their umbrella organization, the AUCC.[3] Despite efforts to intertwine activities, neither side in the equation appeared willing to give up any part of its autonomy for the sake of integration of purpose.

A recent DFAIT study identified the weaknesses inherent in an essentially anarchic situation.[4] They included, among others the following: a) poor coordination and coherence in government policy and programs, both at the federal level and between the federal government and the provinces; b) little investment and marketing in international activities; c) concentration on the Third World and neglect in relation to the industrialized countries; d) no strategy for building on strengths; e) vague international policies within institutions; f) no coherence on tuition fees for foreign students; g) limited offerings in foreign language courses; h) low faculty and student mobility; i) limited appreciation of the influence of cultural factors on teaching, learning and research; and most significantly, j) no sense of urgency about the need to coordinate policy in support of globalization.

In order to overcome these weaknesses, the Report suggested a policy framework that would encourage dialogue and collaborative ventures among Canadian universities, and clearly targeted areas of research with foreign countries and institutions; increased level of awareness and activity abroad with respect of Canada and its strengths; facilitation of faculty and student mobility; developing of partnerships between universities and government, NGOs and business sectors; closer collaboration between the federal and provincial governments through the auspices of the Canadian Education Council, which represents all provincial ministers; regular inter-departmental meetings of government departments and agencies concerned with higher education.

For its part, the Mexican, and more broadly Latin American context, was until recently similarly underfocused, as targets of foreign policy thrusts; this despite the considerable economic, social and even political connections between Canadian and Latin American organisms and individuals.[5] Not until December 1989 did Canadian take a seat in the OAS. It was only then that analysts saw an open opportunity for Canada to develop closer ties with the Western Hemisphere beyond the U.S. in various realms, including higher education.[6] Finally, and most significant for our purposes here, the introduction of the FTA, initiated by Canada, was followed rapidly by the NAFTA, which, while not initiated by Canada, was embraced by the Mulroney government primarily as a means of extending Canada's thirst for multilateral trade and partnerships.[7]

Indeed, it was Mulroney whose famous call following his election to office in 1994 that "Canada is now open for business" propelled trade to the apex of Canada's foreign policy. Whether in the form of its traditionally preferred multilateral arrangements, or through strengthened bilateral partnerships, Canada entered the era where, as an observer put it in relation to the Third World, it underwent a "marked shift of basic altitudes away from liberal internationalism and toward a realism that is narrowly national, preoccupied with economic objectives."[8] The current Liberal government under Jean Chretien has continued the new path with lesser emphasis on traditional themes such as on human rights, development and even peace-keeping than on trade. The Prime Minister has already embarked on several world missions with what he refers to as "Team Canada" consisting of provincial premiers and appropriate business people.

The thing that has not changed dramatically during the past decade is the role of the state in defining Canada's foreign policy. In a provocative recent article in Canada's premier academic international affairs journal, Peter McKenna argues convincingly that Canada's policy toward Latin America follows a clear statist approach.[9] Policy initiatives in this area, he asserts, have been taken with very little consideration to societally-based demands for change in strategy. In supporting this theory, McKenna echoes comments made forcibly by an earlier author, Richard Nossal, who had suggested an elitist interpretation of Canadian foreign policy.[10] Essentially, the argument is made that specific branches within the DFAIT, often in close interdepartmental collaboration with appropriate associated ministries, nudged politicians toward a new Latin American strategy. To quote McKenna "the very initiative for embarking on a review of Canada's policy toward the reform was hatched by one or two officials in the Latin American and Caribbean Branch and not as a response to entreaties from the corporate sector or the non-governmental community."[11]

If our line of reasoning thus far has merit, it would seem that Canadian universities needed to make themselves more central to existing foreign policy concerns. This linkage has come about through what is commonly referred to as globalization and internationalization. Although we cannot be detained here by the manifestations of this phenomenon,[12] it is clear that observers, universities and other related lobbies have been arguing increasingly about the economic benefits accruing to nation states whose educational systems compete successfully in the international marketplace.[13] For example, the 1995 foreign policy review, treated later in this paper, received numerous briefs indicating the value of education to Canada's trade ("education is trade").[14] This, in addition to other more traditional intangible benefits such as "increased domestic mobility and the improvements of standards of higher education.[15] In a similar vein, the government statement, also examined later, declared that Canadian culture (and education) deserve to be a pillar of our foreign policy, "not only because culture...is a major contributor to our economy, but also because [it] expresses internationally the uniqueness of our country."[16] There is little doubt that an expanded role for higher education abroad has been perceived as intimately linked to economic considerations motives and that Canadian higher education institutions in general have decided to take up the challenge of marketing their services.

The Role of Mexico in the New Axis

It is revealing that the primary leadership for the initial trilateral NAFTA contacts of higher education institutions was provided by the respective government agencies. Coinciding with the broader NAFTA negotiations, the DFAIT, along with the Mexican Secretaría de Educación Pública and the U.S. Information Agency, established task forces on higher education and held two trilateral conferences, Wingspread in 1992 and Vancouver in 1993. The former conference brought together government and higher education representatives; the latter was more towardly representative and included the business and other sectors deemed important as potential strategic partners. This is not the place to report on the outcomes of these symposia.[17] What is important for our purposes is to emphasize the governmental initiative in getting these under way and to note that they were both accompanied by a flurry of activity on the part of institutions and umbrella organizations to exploit the new relationship in the higher education sector.

In Canada, the new partner, Mexico, has proven more attractive than the more traditional ally. A recent study commissioned by the AUCC investigated directly both the present ties that Canadian universities have with various world regions as well the desire on the part of the institutions to develop future ties.[18] As Figure 1 indicates, current ties with Mexico and the U.S. rank fourth, after Asia-Pacific, Latin America, and the EC. More significant, however, the largest number of university officials indicated that Mexico ranked first as a priority region (or country) for future university links, outpacing even the very attractive Asia-Pacific connection. The U.S., on the other hand, was deemed third lowest priority area.

Source: J. Knight, Internationalization at Canadian Universities: The Changing Landscape (Ottawa: AUCC, 1995), p. 35.

In light of this phenomenal finding, and under the auspices of DFAIT, the AUCC undertook another survey of Canadian universities later in 1995[19] with two broad objectives: to gauge their interest in promoting educational services in Mexico and to solicit their views on the best ways to effect such a promotion. Of forty-three universities that responded thirteen showed that Mexican ties were of the highest priority for research and academic programs and a total of 31 gave them moderately high to high priority. Very significantly, 34 universities answered affirmatively to the question "does your institution intend to become more involved in the Mexican market?"

The primary objective of the survey was to facilitate holding an "educational fair" in Mexico. Although there was a substantial favourable response, none has been scheduled for the near future.

A recent survey carried out by the Canada-U.S. Fulbright Program, found a total of 337 projects currently involving Canadian universities and colleges in research and study with a focus on both or one of the two NAFTA partners. Of these, 100 had a trilateral and 107 a bilateral concentration (with 86 percent at university level). Given that the author of the report admits that there was a low rate of institutional return, major disciplinary gaps and a slightly better than 60 percent rate of usable responses, it is likely that the number of possible contacts between individuals and institutional in the three countries is much larger.[20] The Program is planning to carry out a more comprehensive survey in the future.

One may only hypothesize about the meaning of these developments. To Canadian universities, the challenge implied in NAFTA consists of becoming better acquainted with a new country, who presents, through relative geographical proximity and a new economic partnership, an interesting and somewhat still exotic prospect for closer collaboration, as a means of counterbalancing the "colossus to the south." As a newly industrialized country with an enormously developed culture, many Canadian universities see collaboration with Mexico as mutually beneficial. Several university officials interviewed by this writer for a study that included collaboration with Mexico, Chile and Argentina, indicated that Mexico, as well as other developed Latin American countries, presented greater possibility of true equal partnerships than those involved in either ODA relationships (for example, Africa), or those of the advanced country of the EC or the U.S. and even the Pacific Rim, where the relationship was one of greater imbalance favouring one side or the other.[21] Regardless of the reasons, the fact remains that collaboration between Canadian and Mexican institutions have grown substantially during the past three years.

The "New" Canadian Foreign Policy and Convergence

The most momentous decision affecting the future of globalizing of higher education in Canada came in February 1995 when the government issued a formal statement asserting new directions in foreign policy. Given the importance of this decision, it is necessary to provide some background to the way in which culture and higher education became an important new pillar of Canadian foreign policy.

In March 1994, the Minister of Foreign Affairs requested the appointment of a Joint Committee of the House of Commons and the Senate to consider Canada's foreign policy. This committee held numerous hearings over the next six months.[22] University Presidents, AUCC, the CBIE, and numerous individuals supported the elevation of culture and post-secondary education to a higher level of recognition by the Canadian government. They indicated, among other things, that Canada was far less generous in its support for academic initiatives than both Mexico and the U.S. Indeed, the Committee learned that Canada in 1993 spent $3.10 per capita on international culture, science and education, compared to $12.60 for Japan and $26.60 for France. Canada's capacity to "address the strategic importance of the internationalization of higher education would enable it to compete in the global economy."

The Committee's recommendations to the government on this very matter became part of a full chapter entitled "Projecting Canadian Culture and Learning Abroad." Aside from standard approval for enhanced scholarships and exchange programs, faculty mobility, institutional exchanges and formation of research and development networks, and the endorsement of many of the recommendations of the draft departmental report, two related recommendations stand out in their directness: that "international cultural, scientific and educational affairs should be treated as a fundamental dimension of Canadian foreign policy" and that the development by the Canadian government take place "with the collaboration of interested provinces of a strategy for Canada's international cultural, scientific and education relations."[23]

The government response to these recommendations came in February 1995, less than three months after the presentation of the Joint Committee report.[24] It stated that Canada would henceforth focus its foreign policy on three objectives: promoting prosperity and employment, protecting its security within a stable global framework, and projecting Canadian values and culture. The government adopted all of the Committee's recommendations on the area of culture and education and confirmed its intention to participate actively in the development of a global information society, as well as to promote Canadian educational products, sciences and expertise as an integral part of the government's International Business Development Program.

As a manifestation of its interest in making cultural and educational affairs an integral part of its foreign policy agenda, DFAIT created in September 1995 a new division named Promotion of Cultural

Industries and Educational Goods and Services. The reader should note the economic appellations accompanying the terms culture and education, an indication of the importance attached to the international trade components of the thrust as well as the effort to steer away from being associated with what are characteristically provincial areas of jurisdiction. In a second initiative, the HRDC in December 1995, which under its former Minister Lloyd Axworthy (now Minister of Foreign Affairs) became a close partner with DFAIT, has approached both the university and private sectors with a view to develop a consortium of these three parties to promote Canadian education abroad. A preliminary meeting of the prospective partners is scheduled for March 1996.[25]

While these initiatives related to emphasizing the importance of international education in general, three other undertakings are more specific to the Mexican connection, both led by DFAIT. The first deals with the organization of a trade fair relating to education (Edu Canada) which took place at the Canadian Business Centre in March 1995 in Mexico City. Designed to enhance opportunities for Canadian institutions to attract Mexican students to their English and French as second language summer programs. The number of Mexican students taking advantage of these programs has been estimated at 15,000.[26] Although the Canadian Business Centre will close in 1996, Edu Canada will host another trade fair in March 1996.

The second enterprise contemplated is the establishment of a Cultural Educational Centre in Mexico, akin to the six already underway in Pacific Rim countries. These centres serve as marketing instruments, designed to attract foreign students to Canadian higher education institutions.

A third major NAFTA-related initiative taken in 1995, and involving the Canadian government deserves special treatment: the implementation of the Program for North American Mobility in Higher Education, jointly sponsored and executed by the federal departments of HRDC and DFAIT. Defined as the Canadian component of the program already in effect in both the U.S. and Mexico, it is intended "to support the development of international joint projects between universities, colleges and technical institutions in the three countries, strengthen cooperation in post-secondary education training and internship and increase undergraduate student mobility."[27] With a budget of Can. $1.3 million over three years, the program provides that all funds be used for student mobility (namely, other types of collaborative projects, including research and faculty mobility are not included). Eleven projects were awarded in the first competition, and affected nineteen Canadian institutions as well as a similar number of

Mexico and US colleges and universities. The contents of the projects varied, but many had clearly a business orientation, ranging from placement for students in internship programs, to the development of common curricula, standards and accreditation for field such as marine biology, architecture, environment, agribusiness and engineering.[28]

Conclusion

The arguments presented in this paper are based on several critically related propositions: first, that trade has grown in importance as the chief objective of Canadian foreign policy; second, that this policy appears to be developed not so much by societal demand, as by internally-driven needs and by statist forces; third that the impulse toward globalization and internationalization within Canadian universities has gained momentum during the past five years and is clearly dominated by a desire to develop mutually advantageous relationships, with governments, with other universities and with the private sector; fourth, that as relative newcomers to the debate on the economic relevance of learning and dispersion of knowledge, Canadian universities have clearly opted to become active partners in international trade; fifth, that as a consequence of the NAFTA relationship, Mexican universities have become very desirable associates; sixth, that once the goals of Canadian universities and the government converge, as they increasingly appear to be on internationalization efforts, the voice of Canadian universities may become more effective in the development of foreign policy; seventh, however, that the Canadian government is still clearly setting the academic agenda abroad.

Two corollaries remain to be alluded to: first, that Canadian universities and the post-secondary education sector in general stand to gain significantly from the relationship and that, therefore, links with Mexican universities and the private sector will likely expand in all areas, including perhaps even those without a direct or immediate economic benefit. Second, that Canadian universities, which have only recently began to consolidate international partnerships with the government and business sectors, will have to make difficult decisions regarding the importance of purely economic considerations in their desire to enter into new arrangements. Regardless of the outcome of these considerations, it is clear that NAFTA has proved to be a catalyst of enormous significance for the new partners, particularly Mexico and Canada, and that higher education has now become a useful tool of Canadian foreign policy.

References

1 * I wish to thank Mr. Joe Moffatt, of DFAIT, Mr. Jean Labrie, of AUCC and my colleague Dr. John Mallea, for drawing my attention to unpublished information.
This paper emphasizes the role of universities. Community colleges are also very active in Mexico and the U.S., primarily through the auspices of ACCC. To a great extent, the arguments made are valid for the whole of higher education the issue of "culture" lies outside the perimeters of this study (please see below for acronyms).

2 T. Keating, Canada and the World Order (Toronto: McLelland & Stewart, 1993).

3 Other Canadian associations that are very active include CERLAC, CALACS, FOCAL, CAMS, IOHE and the Canada-U.S. Fulbright program.

4 DFAIT "The International Dimension of Higher Education in Canada" (Ottawa: DFAIT, 1994).

5 See J.C.M. Ogelsby, Gringos From the Far North (Toronto: MacMillan, 1976).

6 E. Dosman "Canada and Latin America: The New Look" in International Journal, XLVII, 3 (Summer 1992), pp. 529-54.

7 Keating, op. cit., p. 240-44.

8 C. Pratt " Canada: An Eroding and Limited Internationalism" in C. Pratt, ed. Internationalism Under Strain (Toronto: University of Toronto Press, 1989), p. 59.

9 See McKenna "Canada's Policy Towards Latin America: A Statist Interpretation" in International Journal, XLIX, 4 (Autumn, 1994), pp. 929-53 for details.

10 K.R. Nossal, The Politics of Canadian Foreign Policy (Scarborough, ON: Prentice-Hall, 1985).

11 McKenna, op. cit., p. 951.

12 For an excellent summary of trends and analysts on internationalization, see J. Mallea "The Internationalization of Higher Education: Stakeholder Views in North America," unpublished manuscript, 1995.

13 Mallea, op. cit., pp. 6-11, cites the work of Head, Kennedy, Reich, Therrow and in North America, Porter (The Competitive Advantage of Nations), as seminal in the area of higher education as a trading partner.

14 Comment made by J. Fox, Executive Director of CBIE to the Report of the Joint Committee of Parliament, Canada's Foreign Policy: Principles and Priorities for the Future (Ottawa, 1994), p. 64. See also AUCC "Canadian Universities: Stakeholders in Canada's Foreign Policy" and "Globalization: Challenges and Opportunities for Canadian Universities,"

unpublished, undated position paper, ca. 1993.

15 Joint Committee, op. cit., p. 65.

16 Government of Canada, Canada in the World; Government Statement (Ottawa, 1995), p. 8.

17 See Wingspread, "North American Higher Education Cooperation: Identifying the Agenda (Racine, WIS: The Johnson Foundation, 1992) and Worldstat International "North American Higher Education Cooperation: Implementing the Agenda" (Mississauga, ON, 1993). A third conference, planned in Guadalajara, Mexico for April 1996, has as its title "Partners for Prosperity" and emphasizes the workforce, research transfer, academic and professional mobility, corporate-higher education partnerships. See the draft conference announcement by (DFAIT, 1996).

18 J. Knight "Internationalization at Canadian Universities: The Changing Landscape" (Ottawa: AUCC, 1995).

19 " Canadian University Survey: Marketing in Mexico?" (Ottawa: AUCC, 1995).

20 V. Konrad "Research and Study of North America: The Canadian Dimension" (Ottawa: The Canada-U.S. Fulbright Program, 1995).

21 M. Serfaty "The Promotion of Canadian Universities in Mexico, Argentina and Chile" (Ottawa: AUCC, 1994).

22 See Report, op. cit.

23 Ibid., pp. 61-71.

24 "Government Response to the Recommendations of the Special Joint

25 Parliamentary Committee Reviewing Canadian Foreign Policy" (Ottawa: Government of Canada, 1995), esp. pp. 76-91).

26 Information provided by Mr. Jean Labrie, AUCC.

27 "Edu Canada '96" (Ottawa: DFAIT & CBIE, 1996).

28 "Program for North American Mobility in Higher Education: Guidelines" (Ottawa: Government of Canada, 1995).

"Backgrounder: Program for North American Mobility in Higher Education: Projects Announced" (Ottawa: HRDC, 1995).

Acronyms

ACCC:	Association of Community Colleges of Canada
AUCC:	Association of Universities and Colleges of Canada
CALACS:	Canadian Association for Latin American and Caribbean Studies
CAMS:	Canadian Association of Mexican Studies
CBIE:	Canadian Bureau for International Education
CERLAC:	Centre for Research on Latin America and the Caribbean
DFAIT:	Department of Foreign Affairs and International Trade (a federal government department)
EC:	European Community
FTA:	Free Trade Agreement (Canada-U.S.)
HRDC:	Human Resources Development Canada
IACS:	International Association of Canadian Studies
IOHE:	Inter-American Organization for Higher Education
NGO:	Non-Governmental Organization
OAS:	Organization of American States
ODA:	Overseas Development Assistance

Chapter VII

Nafta and California Proposition 187: ¿Hegemony or Cultural & Political Hypocrisy?

Gillermo Rojas

To the Mexican intelligentsia NAFTA, (North American Free Trade Agreement) or TLC (El Tratado de Libre Comercio) as it is known in Mexico, is a treaty of equality between three trading partners, Mexico, the United States and Canada. The California politics of Proposition 187 targets Mexican illegals and violates the spirit of cooperation, for after all, the treaty permits free trade and movement of commodities and labor is one of those commodities. Mexicans view California's Proposition 187 as hypocritical in light of the fact that California shared the largest of the trade exchanges between the two countries in 1995.

In cultural studies and the study of discourses in society, one theorizes that social and political entities exist for their own self preservation and self reproduction.

The powers to be reproduced themselves socially and culturally; their families and their friends form primarily ruling elites that control the seats of power, but in their midst there are many different sectors which create a dissonance and a counter force to the ruling elites. These dialectics and political dynamics are constant, and in these post-modern times the conflicts are almost instantaneous and simultaneous to the events as they occur.

NAFTA is a product of Clinton's politics. NAFTA enhances the national economics. Proposition 187 is Pete Wilson's politics; he claims illegal immigrants drain the state treasury and Washington does not return enough dollars to remedy the California deficit produced by the downturn of military base closings, cuts in defense contracts and layoffs in the major weapon producing companies of Southern California. Illegal immigrants can not vote. Unemployed personnel do vote. Both politicians and voters need a scapegoat. The illegals are, and have always been, targets of scapegoating when the economy does not produce enough jobs.

Both Americans and Mexicans have addressed the negative and the positive aspects of California Proposition 187 in the California elections of November 1994.

Both have seen it as a racist proposition; Californians want to secure their borders from Mexicans. Mexicans see it as a negative and discriminatory measure which will put the burden of proof on citizens born of Mexican parents in the United States. The burden of proof of citizenship will bring out a discriminatory and unequal treatment based on their race and ethnicity. Both perspectives carry some truth as we shall see.

Electoral Votes

On Tuesday, November 7, 1994 fifty-nine percent of the California voting electorate supported California Proposition 187. Forty-one percent voted against the measure known as the "Save our state" measure. The proposition was designed to deny education, social services and health services to illegal immigrants and their children in order to save the tax payers from the burdens of taxation.

Political facts

Pete Wilson was running for reelection to his second term as Governor of the state of California and in the four years of his tenure the state had not recovered from its profound recession and its loss of "730,000 jobs and the massive defense cutbacks during the last five years." (LA Times, (Jan. 1995) Pete Wilson knew all these facts in the 1994 campaign, but he chose to suppress these facts and look at the issues of "fear" and "demagoguery." Wilson decided to blame the illegals and the poor who according to repeated pronouncements cost the state precious resources. All through his reelection campaign

Governor Pete Wilson never said a word about the fact that 200 dollars a week of unemployment compensation for each worker would cost the state 146 million dollars a week. In ten weeks it would be 1.46 billion dollars. Compensation for each worker runs out at the end of 26 weeks, so the state would have to pick up 3 billion dollars cost. This had nothing to do with the illegal immigrants, yet not once did Wilson choose to make these facts public. On the other hand the illegal immigrants were the ones working and paying taxes to provide the weekly revenue for the high-tech unemployed workers. Wilson never said a word. Technology permits us to claim a truth with only a portion of the facts. Wilson was in a political campaign and had to provide a galvanizing slogan and platform to get reelected. Fear of illegals was translated into the rhetoric of Proposition 187 and fear of criminals was translated into Proposition 184. The two slogans masked the prejudices against the two targeted groups. Both groups have a material and economic consequence that goes far beyond the veiled political sloganeering which comes out with every election. These slogans drove the California people to the voting polls. Those are the basic political facts of proposition 187 and the November 1994 reelection campaign of Governor Pete Wilson.

Racial considerations in the campaign

The anti-proposition 187 forces were characterized as "Mexican Lovers" and "Beaners." No matter how hard the Wilson forces denied the racist and xenophobic innuendoes, there were many who were overt in their racist position. The epithets of "Mexican lovers" and "beaners" clearly were racist and were referents marked for targeting the working-class Mexicans whose primary diets of beans and tortillas have been studied by anthropologists and known since the domestication of corn. Beans and exotl, ejote (green beans) are well-known indices of the Mexican indegenous diet. The epithets, "beaners" excluded the other immigrants:Thai, Chinese and other Asian nationalities. The epithets clearly were directed at Mexico. This should remind us of the 1936-1938 deportations of Mexicans. At that time the same hate-fear tactics were used to deport many legal Mexican-American citizens. These fears were evident throughout the campaign, before and after the vote. It is interesting to note that the deportations and vilification of Mexicans in 1936-1938 and Proposition 187 in 1994 took place when the economies had gone sour. In the first instance it was the national economy, in the latter it was the California economy with 730,000 lost jobs due to the closing of military bases and closing of arm productions.

Fear and hypocrisy in the 1994 elections played a major role in the campaign. Pete Wilson and his political strategists were not happy with one hate-fear strategy, they coupled the "illegal immigrant proposition" to the "three strikes, you are out" criminal proposition. When you juxtapose the two, you can see clearly that the campaign from the very beginning was targeting two groups of "non-voters," undocumented workers and incarcerated African-Americans. As non-voters, they became the "scapegoats." A year after the election, the "International Report" in its Dec. 1995 edition wrote: "Nationwide Proposition 187 gained the most publicity, however it was but one of twenty-two bills in the California state legislature based on racialized premises. Although Proposition 187 and the twenty-two bills focused on 'illegals,' in reality the blame encompassed a much broader population in the popular mind such that legal and "ilegal" immigrants of Mexico, citizens of Mexican descent virtually all Latinos, and Mexican nationals, were conflated within the blurred and sloppy logic that is the trademark of political scapegoating. Pro-Proposition187 activists envisioned a war to keep the U.S. from being overrun by 'immigrant hordes:' "It boils down to this," stated the founder of the anti-immigrant group Voice of Citizens Together, "Do we want to retain control of the Southwest more than the Mexicans want to take it away from us?" (International Report, Dec. 1995, 5-6).

Linking Proposition 187 and Proposition 184, which advocated mandatory incarcerations for three-time felons, permitted Wilson's campaign to associate Mexicans with African-Americans and other criminal elements. The two propositions were targeting racial groups. Proposition 184 requested additional funding for building more prisons while cutting budgets for education, social services and medical services. The political and cultural hypocrisy was evident the day that Gov. Pete Wilson, Senate candidate Michael Huffington and other Republicans "exhorted a faithful crowd in the San Gabriel Valley city of Monrovia to vote for Proposition 184, the tough 'three strikes and you're out' sentencing measure on the ballot. Wilson said a strong affirmative vote for Proposition 184 is essential tomorrow even though an identical measure passed the Legislature and was signed into law this year (1994)."

It is important to note four things: 1) Why the redundancy of the political action on the part of Governor Wilson, Michael Huffington, and the other Republicans?; 2) Why would the political leaders spend financial resources on a criminal measure which was already an enacted law and a legislated statute in the books?; 3) What is the motivation (or the political gains) of saturating the political air waves with a measure that has already been delivered as a measure of security to the voters? 4) Why would Wilson inflame the campaign rhetoric with an issue which was already a moot issue? The California State Legislature had passed a law which demonstrated to the voters that the legislature was getting tough with criminals. This measure had been achieved by a non-partisan vote but Wilson rhetoricized a moot issue to get the attention of the voters and pander to the voters' fears. Wilson was a true demagogue and his motive was to inflame the voters to consider the other twenty-two bills which he presented for his own political gains, the state's governorship. The legislature already legally had inscribed the penalties for the three-time felons, but it was not sufficient for Pete Wilson who wanted to make sure the California electorate would turn out in November to vote their hatred, their fears, and their concerns for safety. My criticism and observations of Pete Wilson do not in any way minimize the serious problem of criminal activity and danger of shootings on the California streets. Rather my observations are made to focus on how Governor Wilson successfully yoked the racial and economic strategies on the backs of Mexicans and African Americans. By not reporting the true unemployment figures, by scapegoating Mexicans and African-Americans, Governor Wilson knowingly and willingly created an identity with the voters' economic fears and fears of criminals. (This was not the first time Republicans had used such a tactic. Republicans had blamed Michael Dukakis for the release of Willie Horton, African-American criminal. The advertisement suggested that Democrats were soft on crime, and Republicans were tough.) Californians in great numbers attributed directly the state's economic downturn on the use of California social services which were being drained not by illegals, but by the unemployed in the military procurement sector which was running at 146 million dollars per week. After 26 weeks these workers went off the unemployment records radar and were no longer tracked. It is not a coincidence that the Republicans chose to make the redundancy case work out for their unstated fear of the illegals. The hypocritical contradictory motivations are not totally clear. On the one hand the Republicans argued that the illegal immigrants were a drain on the resources provided for education, health and other services. No research exists which documents this loss of revenues. On the contrary it stands to reason that the loss of tax revenue generated by the undocumented workers will produce an even greater drain on the state tax resources, for through their work they pay the cost of unemployment compensation by the thousands who are still unemployed from the military procurement. In addition these illegal workers pay rent which is inscribed for taxes. They pay gasoline, cigarette and liquour taxes. All of these pay for improvements in the infrastructure, roads, bridges etc. Those who argue that they do not pay property taxes used to pay for education, the illegal workers pay rent which has a tax cost passed off by the property owner. Illegal workers do pay their share. One needs to reflect on the fact that demagogic and political rhetoric is invented for winning elections and not for explaining political and economic realities.

What is even more hypocritical is the fact that the loss of U.S. defense contracts and the closing of military bases produced enormous unemployment rolls and yet Wilson kept all of these facts from the political campaign. The Federal Government's policy to close military bases and the loss of U.S. defense contracts produced a huge down turn in the California economy and produced the enormous California deficit. Pete Wilson was duplicitous when he attempted to blame the California economic downturn on the education cost of 300,000 children of illegal immigrants or the social services delivered to 1.3 million or 2.0 million illegal immigrants. (There is no certainty of the numbers and to this day no one knows what is the total number of illegal immigrants in California).

As we now know the campaign based on willful and calculated racist messages was successful. The final analysis of the vote revealed that 59% of the voting electorate had supported Proposition 187 and 41% had voted against the measure.

Hypocrisy at the highest levels

Pete Wilson, mayor of San Diego, and U.S. Senator for California, represented San Diego politics for more than fifteen years. Pete Wilson and every City Council member knows San Diego's urbanization and its dependency on U.S. defense contracts dates from 1894. These facts are all a matter of San Diego's history and city politics. Pete Wilson is a hypocrite when he ignores the loss of federal moneys and the relationship to the major unemployment crisis and its direct relationship to the California deficit.

Roger Lotchin's "Fortress California 1910-1960: From Warfare to Welfare" extrapolated significant political and economic data which presents a more reasonable scenario that explains the root of the current economic crisis in California. Roger Lotchin in "Fortress California" studies how U.S. military defense budgets have been the major industrial-manufacturing drive in California's modern history. As early as 1854, says Lotchin, "the United States government created the Navy Yard at Vallejo, and from at least that time onward, American

Urban California was aware of the uses of military patronage for city boosting." (p. 1) The City of San Diego fought for the Washington appropriations in what Lotchin calls "possession of the sailors." (p. 6) Lotchin describes how "this naval realignment triggered economic war up and down the West Coast, as San Diego, Los Angeles, Seattle, Vallejo, and San Francisco" fought over the U.S. Defense naval appropriations.

The earliest wrangling over the Washington handouts took place in 1919. Fifteen years later, the San Diego Union reports: "Today San Diego boasts a total capital investment of $28,000,000 in naval establishments, with an annual naval payroll of $30,000,000 [of an "annual naval appropriation" of $300,000,000]. We should protect this great investment and keep this vital payroll. . ." (p. 3) This payroll was 30 percent of San Diego's annual payroll. As the U.S. naval fleet found new homes on the Pacific, the U.S. defense dollars followed. Metropolitan leaders were already creating a political and economic marriage of their cities and the U.S. department of defense. Lotchin states: "The marriage of the city and the sword in California was a voluntary rather than a shotgun affair. Lotchin also states that city boosters of San Francisco, San Diego, Oakland and Vallejo developed a "doctrine of industrial advantages." World War I had produced an economic boom: "Extractive industries like fishing, mining, lumbering, and agriculture boomed along with shipbuilding. These activities brought marked prosperity to California cities and to new migrants like the Mexicans as well. However, the boom collapsed after the war, leaving a trail of economic dislocation behind it. The newly founded aircraft industry folded, shipbuilding declined dramatically, and the extractive industries fell off significantly as well. The war also produced serious inflation, profiteering, and social tension. Labor unrest was a serious problem from at least 1916 to the census year, and both radicalism and antiradicalism flared up along with it. The economy did not fully right itself until 1921." (Lotchin, 5-6)

It is inconceivable that Pete Wilson would have explained the 1980's California economic crisis with these historical facts and the loss of 600,000 jobs in the 1980's due to the closing of military bases and loss of federal defense contracts. To have done so would be an admission that the political dependency on the Pentagon and the federal budget cuts were the direct cause of the deficit. The voters would have had no scapegoat to blame for the California economic misery. Wilson was out to get the votes of the military personnel, the state and federal employees, whose taxes had gone up and whose employment skills had been laid off because of the shrinking federal defense dollars. Wilson had to find a scapegoat just as other politicians had scapegoated the Mexicans Immigrants in the 1930's. Governor Pete Wilson targeted the hate and fears of the California electorate as a sure way to reelection.

The scapegoating of Mexicans reminds us that in 1936-1938, during another historical economic downturn in the United States, the same hate-fear tactics were used to deport many legal Mexican-American citizens. These fears were evident then as well as through the California 1994 campaign. The Mexicano and Latino community reacted in many ways: 1) Students demonstrated in the high schools and the universities; 2) Some high school students chose to walkout of their classes creating a major rift in the anti-proposition 187 forces. The teachers and social workers supported the anti-proposition 187 vote. Since the student walkouts were producing a drain on funds returned to schools based on days attended, the students were persuaded to return to classes; 3) Truck drivers while in their vehicles demonstrated support of the student strikes and other demonstrations by sounding their horns in support; 4) The radio, the press and television challenged the supporters of the proposition in many daily programs; 5) The community social workers and other labor union officials also supported the anti-proposition 187 vote by calling for demonstrations.

Federal Government Interventionism or Federal Funds before Prop 187

In 1990 the federal government granted California 115.8 billion dollars. ("The Book of the States," 1992-1993 edition, 422) Using Herbert Wulf's "Arms Industry Limited" figures in which the global arms industry will shrink by 20-30% in the short and the long run, it is not difficult to understand how the weapons-industrial and military complex has shrunk since the days of Michael Gorbachov and Perestroika. Wulf and his Stockholm International Peace Research Institute (SIPRI) colleagues estimate that all the armament factories in the world will dislocate 30% of their workers. When one reviews carefully California Cities and the Sword, and the story of urbanization, the story of weapons manufacturing, the story of political hunger for military bases, a story of growth and endless possibilities and one then juxtaposes the horrific downsizing story of the global arms industry as Wulf and his SIPRI colleagues project, one begins to contemplate conservatively a 20% of 115.8 billion; these downsizing figures for California present a loss of 23.16 billion dollars. These are major budgetary dislocations in a state such as California where for

100 years the urbanization of California has taken place on the backs of Washington Defense contracts. Wilson never told the voters these horrendous and painful future outlooks. Rather Governor Wilson took the low road of finding non-voting scapegoats, illegal immigrants and prison inmates. The reader must keep in mind that the real hemorrage on the state budget is being produced by the numbers of laid off procurement workers, by the mortgage institutions whose tax dollars are affected by home buyers who can no longer pay, by workers declaring bankruptcy, by small companies going under. The deficit is being created by an economic reversal never seen in California state politics.

California political kingpins prepared the racial and discriminatory rhetoric of proposition 187 one year before the vote taken on Tuesday, November 7, 1994. The political wisdom of the supporters relied on the old notion that the immigrants were to blame for the California economic recession that the state was experiencing. This sophomoric and naive perspective of scapegoating the immigrants reveals Pete Wilson's historical and cultural myopia which denied the economic roots of California's economic downturn.

Political scapegoating

America's history of blaming the immigrants has a long standing evolution. During the seventeenth century the American revolutionists blamed the British royalists for not supporting the efforts of breaking away from the British Crown. Many of these were Irish immigrants. The early settlers blamed the Irish of Boston for many political and economic reversals in the seventeenth and eighteenth centuries. The Irish of New York blamed the Italians who did not speak English. The Italians and Irish have blamed the Jewish immigrants. And the list goes on. American political figures have always found the immigrants easy targets of their scapegoating. The immigrants at all times are easy prey because they have not yet acculturated to their new country and have not yet learned the democratic process nor have they acquired the political knowledge with which to fight back and declare their class and ethnic interests. All of the immigrants in America have been at risk of being scapegoated when the economy has gone sour.

Hypocrisy from the White House

On Monday, November 7, 1994, the day before the election, President Bill Clinton traveled to California to support a number of democratic candidates running for California state offices. While he made speeches, Pete Wilson criticized President Clinton for causing the three billion dollar deficit produced by the large number of illegal immigrants in California. During this visit Wilson blamed President Bill Clinton for contributing to the California budget problems.

Clinton retorted that Pete Wilson while serving as Senator for California had supported legislative measures which had produced these deficits: Clinton said, "For the governor [Pete Wilson] to say, 'Here's a hole in the budget and you fix it' when the hole was created in part by federal policies he helped to enact, is a little disingenuous, ... when I'm the first person who tried to help him." (The Times Mirror Company Los Angeles Times, Nov. 7, 1994, A1).

Pete Wilson stated that President Clinton's remarks were "election-year cosmetics," and in another instance that Clinton's campaigning in California "has been pathetic." (The Times Mirror Company Los Angeles Times, Nov. 7, 1994, A1).

Clinton in a televised interview "acknowledged that the costs of illegal immigration are a federal responsibility, but he sharply disputed the Republican governor's estimate of $3 billion a year." Furthermore President Clinton claimed he did not know how "that amount could be determined." (The Times Mirror Company Los Angeles Times, Nov. 7, 1994, A1).

It is at this point that the hypocritical masks on the part of both state and federal governments begin to come off. One, if the illegal immigrants are in the country, how then does one keep count of their numbers and the costs of the supposed services they use? Clinton attacked Pete Wilson when he explained how the problem in California has been produced on the backs of earlier decisions by both state and federal government officials.

Clinton states: "The governor has said California would not have a budget deficit if the federal government lived up to its congressional mandate to compensate the state. Wilson's critics accuse him of being part of the problems because of legislation he sponsored while in the U.S. Senate to allow immigrants to enter California as farm workers." (The Times Mirror Company Los Angeles Times, Nov. 7, 1994, A1)

Again hypocrisy looms high on the horizon. While Pete Wilson served as U.S. Senator from California he supported the immigrants who were coming to work in the agricultural enterprises of California through a series of votes in the U.S. Senate. California agribusiness welcomed the cheap labor and Wilson delivered time after time by votes in the U.S. Senate. As U.S. Senator agribusiness dollars supported Wilson's reelections. As elected governor of California Wilson must balance the state budget. As State Senator he never was responsible for the state budget.

Clinton's dispute and disbelief of the high budget cost of services to the illegal immigrants do not excuse his ignorance of what the real figures are. Here President Clinton and Pete Wilson are both hypocritical when arguing that no one knows. The citizens would argue that both Clinton and Wilson should know, because both Clinton and Wilson are the elected officials who get elected and paid to know.

Clinton further sheds light on the hypocrisy by both Federal and State elected officials. When Clinton criticized the 3 billion dollar figure he stated: "...the reimbursement to the states should be offset, or reduced by an amount equal to the state taxes paid by those illegal immigrants who are working in California. Clinton said he did not know how that amount could be determined."

This is where the hypocrisy really gets thick. President Clinton publicly stated that the immigrants like all other citizens with papers are not exempt from paying taxes. The fact that neither the state nor the federal government has a process by which to track the movement of illegal immigrants and their patterns of paying taxes is not an issue that the immigrants can resolve. They are not in a position to record their tax contributions to the state.

It is indeed a sad commentary for both politicians to ignore the 780,000 lost jobs in the California economy. It is hypocritical for both politicians not to speak to the voters on the impossibility of the federal budget to continue subsidizing the arms race when the entire global world arm manufacturing is down by 25 - 30%. The United States continues to support the building of the Trident submarine on the East Coast only to avoid another California economic downturn. Both Pete Wilson and Bill Clinton have avoided informing the voters of the real cuts and the real sacrifices to which the U.S. citizenry must commit in order to survive in an economy which can no longer produce arms. The metaphor "to turn arms into share plows" is long overdue. The west coast metropolitan communities of San Diego, Long Beach, Vallejo, San Francisco and Seattle, Washington have achieved their growth and development on the backs of the federal government defense budgets.

The base closings and the cuts in defense spending will continue to erode the jobs in all communities historically and politically dependent on the Pentagon. It is hypocritical for politicians to argue that major budget dislocations are the fault of the poorest of the poorest in society, the aged, the children, the poor, the immigrants and the incarcerated. To scapegoat those who do not vote is not "realpolitik."

Bill Clinton and Pete Wilson in their war of words reveal how the immigrants have become political pawns in the elections of 1994 and both, state and federal, officials have revealed their hypocrisy and their transparent public masks suggest an inability to govern or to resolve the contemporary problems facing both state and federal governments.

Pete Wilson's and Bill Clinton's political self-serving statements are poor examples of government and reflect a serious low point in the American political process, one which will endear politicians to their constituencies, but will meet in utter defeat on the economic front. Political and hypocritical posturing on televised programs or the front pages of the American newspapers will not resolve the base closings or the downsizing of the defense budgets. Without a change of heart on the part of the political leaders, American politics in 1996 promises to be a year replete with hypocrisy and vacuous statements. (Postcript: The November 6, 1996 electoral vote turnout was the lowest since 1824).

Part III

Chapter VIII

Giving NAFTA The Silent Treatment: Theories of Foreign Policy-Making and the Accession of Chile

Renee Scherlen

Introduction

Surprising best characterizes 1995, the second year of NAFTA. It was marked by events unanticipated either prior to or following the passage of the Agreement. The predictions of an economic boom for Mexico and the consequential bust for the United States did not take place. In contrast, Mexico has weathered tremendous economic turmoil; the United States apparently has not been boosted by the Agreement nor has the great "sucking noise" of jobs and money draining south occurred. On the whole, there was rising unpopularity, as the Agreement has been plagued by unmet expectations. The treaty has lost its sparkle, even among its initial supporters.

What a contrast to the anticipations for this second year. In the heady days of December 1994, during the Summit of the Americas, NAFTA appeared to be the initial step toward a hemispheric free trade zone. Pledges were made to expand economic cooperation and create a Free Trade Area of the Americas (FTAA); a timetable was established to move the hemisphere forward. And, the first expansion of NAFTA was announced. Chile was selected as the first new member of NAFTA; the first non-North American member. NAFTA was presented as the mechanism for greater economic development in the Americas. As the first year of NAFTA ended, the second year began to take on a dynamic shape: 1995 would see the first steps toward an enlarged NAFTA that would eventually encompass the entire region.

The accession of Chile marked the beginning of a new phase. The three member nations would have to develop foreign policy coordination, particularly if NAFTA was to be the vehicle for the creation of the FTAA.The text of the treaty did not provide much guidance for this; thus, negotiations between Canada, Mexico, and the United States about the pace, scope, and character of accession began--in conjunction with the actual bargaining with Chile.

Yet this expansion of NAFTA has become lost in a deafening silence. Mexico is beset by economic and political crises. These crises in Mexico are raising doubts in the United States about the wisdom of NAFTA. Rather than moving forward toward an ever-expanding Free Trade Area, there is a growing chorus to withdraw from the existing agreement. As one observer noted:

> ... in the coming political season the White House wants Mexico to stay in the closet and, until the Mexican economy gets restarted, is willing to pretend that NAFTA never happened [Whalen 1996: C3].

When public attention does crop up, it focuses primarily on the economic relationship between Mexico and the United States. Little is heard about the Chilean accession. There has been a loss of momentum: a bill authorizing "fast-track" status for Chile's accession failed. Yet, even this legislative defeat did not generate much publicity or media coverage. The subject of NAFTA enlargement has disappeared from public debate.

I argue that this vanishing act is deliberate. The quiet approach is a conscious strategy on the part of the United States government (particularly the executive branch, but including all those favoring NAFTA expansion in the legislative branch as well) to gain control over the accession process within the United States. As an examination of the various models of foreign policy-making reveals, lowering the prominence of an issue reduces the number of political actors involved in the process. The only chance for Chilean accession lies with the depoliticization of the accession process. And the only way to depoliticize NAFTA expansion is to lessen public attention and emphasize the international context of the decision.

This essay argues that the initial passage of NAFTA, as well as the turmoil suffered in Mexico during 1995, chastened proponents of NAFTA expansion. It contends that to achieve their goals, the accession process must proceed in a very different manner than the first NAFTA process: expansionists must shift perceptions about NAFTA in order to gain control over the ratification process and assure successful passage. The paper begins with a brief review of the first legislative battle over NAFTA. Then, it turns to an evaluation of different models of foreign policy-making: after outlining the basic elements of the four main models, the essay situates NAFTA within this theoretical construct. The essay then turns to the issue of how proponents of accession can gain control over NAFTA: expansionists are compelled to lessen the public profile of Chilean accession, shift perceptions about the domestic impact of this economic agreement, and focus on international aspects of the expansion. In addition to identifying the necessary strategy, the paper discusses the implications of these tactics--particularly with reference to potential for success. Finally, the essay concludes with an assessment of how the silent treatment--developed in response to domestic pressures--affects U.S. partners in NAFTA and Chile as well as the future of foreign policy coordination.

The Creation of NAFTA: A Brief Review

Initially, when the notion of a North American Free Trade Agreement first arose, its passage appeared assured. Enjoying bipartisan support, building on an economic accord with Canada that had generated (in the United States) little controversy, the approval of fast-track status seemed to auger smooth sailing. However, the passage of the NAFTA grew into a long, elaborate, multi-dimensional, and multi-actor process. Among the key participants were: the White House (under both Republican Bush and Democrat Clinton), Congress, several executive departments (Commerce, Treasury, Labor, etc); the two main political parties; independent candidates (H. Ross Perot, most notably); labor unions; environmental groups; and other interest groups.

Proponents of NAFTA--despite their overwhelming numbers within the ranks of official Washington--lost control over the process. Indeed, it devolved to the point were it was uncertain whether or not passage would occur up until the moment of the vote. Thus, in spite of relatively strong and broad bipartisan support at the elite level (encompassing two administrations from different political parties as well as prominent Congressional supporters from both parties), NAFTA was a near defeat. Proponents lost of control as number of participants increased, particularly as negative public attention grew. This stands in mark contrast with the experience over the agreement to create a free trade area with Canada, which passed relatively unnoticed, without debate, and no controversy in the United States.

Why was passage of NAFTA so contentious? There are many possible explanations. Essentially, economic union with Canada was perceived as non-threatening. So may attribute this to the relative economic parity between the U.S. and Canada--as compared to the great disparity between the United States and Mexico. Others may argue that while many in the United States are ignorant about both Canada and Mexico, Canada is viewed much more positively than Mexico (based on similarities in language, ethnicity, racial composition, etc). All of these may be true and may have contributed to the environment surrounding the passage of NAFTA. But, part of the explanation lies in the context of the decision-making process. An exploration of the different models of foreign policy making offers a potential explication for why passage of NAFTA spun out of the control of its proponents.

Models of Foreign Policy Making

Investigations of the foreign policy-making process in the United States have resulted in numerous theoretical constructs about how foreign policy gets made. In general, one can identify four main models used to explain the process. Each one has distinct characteristics, participants, and criteria for decision-making. Initially, analysts argued over which model was the correct one: now, students of foreign policy-making concede that circumstances determine which model most accurately details the foreign policy process.

The first model is known either as the rational actor or presidential model. This construct assumes a small number of actors --located primarily within the executive branch-- who analytically weigh the pros and cons of various options and develop the best policy in the national interest of the United States (see Allison 1970 for the classic discussion of this model). As many have noted, this model

> ...suggest foreign policy decision making can be isolated from the political process and based on coolly calculated considerations organized, and proceeds according to the canons of logic, merit, and rational argumentation [Wiarda 1990: 22]

Furthermore, this model postulates an elite-based, elite-driven foreign policy process that --given the small number of participants and the rational basis of decision-making-- is fairly easy to control.

A second model is the administrative or organizational model. This model hypothesizes that many foreign policy decisions arise because of established bureaucratic procedures (known as standard operating procedures-SOPs) and bureaucratic expertise. In essence, this model details a process of foreign policy making that emphasizes routine and lower level actors: it argues that most decisions fall within this category.

> The power of agencies that underlie the administrative model rests on the scope and complexity of foreign policy. ... the myriad international issues and inter-actions in which the national government is involved ... [and] the complicated nature of foreign policy and the specialized knowledge and experience to deal with the host of diplomatic, military, economic, and other U.S. foreign policy concerns [Rourke et al 1994: 149].

The third model is often termed the bureaucratic or sub-governmental model. Drawing upon studies of domestic policy-making, this model argues that foreign policy --like all other types of policy-- is primarily the result of bureaucratic struggles for power, influence, and control. Most often, decisions involve more than one administrative agency: thus, the decision-making process becomes the arena in which differing perceptions, interests, and resources conflict. The model does not assume that the United States government is a single actor; rather, there are multiple positions and "where you stand depends on where you sit" (i.e., what job you hold). In the end, according to this model

> a policy emerges from a process of simultaneous conflict and accommodation among a multitude of [bureaucratic] actors with competing viewpoints and possessing different amounts of power [Spanier and Uslaner 1994: 308-309].

The fourth model is the political process model. This model asserts that foreign policy decision-making is a process that involves the entire spectrum of political actors in the United States. Thus, not only are the White House, Congress, the executive branch important--so are interest groups, the media and public opinion. Underpinning this perspective is the argument that

> foreign policy is often determined in significant part by domestic considerations that have little to do with such lofty concepts as national interest or geo-strategic theory [Rourke et al 1994: 146].

While this echoes sentiments expressed in the bureaucratic/sub-governmental model, the political process model asserts that the number of actors frequently encompasses much more than different agencies or even branches of the government: "foreign policy has been politicized and made the stuff of domestic, political and partisan considerations" [Wiarda 1990: 33].

As suggested above, no one model best describes foreign policy making under all circumstances. Rather, a two by two matrix may be formed and the different models placed into their respective positions. Analyses of various foreign policy decisions indicate that two variables are key when determining the type of policy-making process most applicable: (1) the prominence of an issue and (2) the degree to which an issue is intermestic or international.

A number of factors determine the prominence of an issue. Wide-ranging and intense debates are indications of high prominence. Crisis situations create high prominence, as do non-status quo circumstances (no SOPs to rely on). Issues with high emotional involvement also create high prominence. In addition, symmetry and zero-sum game perceptions are key. Situations were penalties and benefits are unequally distributed (asymmetrical) lead to high prominence. Likewise, perceptions that the policy is zero-sum any benefits entails losers--contribute to high prominence.

Categorizing issues as either intermestic or international can be difficult. Analytically, intermestic issues are those that have a domestic impact; conversely, international issues are those that influence external circumstances only. Of course, very few (if any) policies would strictly adhere to an "international" definition. Thus, as one scholar notes:

> [t]he key to telling which issue is international and which is intermestic is perceived domestic stakes. When the public or specific groups believe that they will be affected by a policy, they tend to become more active politically and to move the issue into the inter-mestic realm [Rourke et al: 158, emphasis in the original].

Thus, if the impact of a policy can be made to appear more removed from the everyday life of an average citizen (or vice versa), then the issue may take on a more international character (or, conversely, intermestic). Table 1 shows the foreign policy model associated with the different mixtures of prominence and issue type.

Table 1

	Intermestic Issue	International Issue
High Prominence	Political Process	Presidential
Low Prominence	Bureaucratic	Administrative

The implications of the foreign policy models, in particular the circumstances that surround which model dominates the policy-making process, are profound. Clearly, the fewer actors involved in decision-making, the greater control exercised over the outcome. Those trying to pass a policy would prefer the presidential model of decision-making; failing this, the preferences would be administrative, then bureaucratic, and finally the political process. Given that perception is central to the type of policy-making process most likely to develop, there is a vested interest in influencing the international/ intermestic label attached to an issue, as well as elements that shape the prominence of a policy.

Using the terminology of the matrix, the economic agreement between Canada and the United States was perceived in the United States as more international than intermestic and enjoyed low prominence: the domestic stakes were thought to be minimal, the situation was perceived to be non-crisis, status quo oriented, with symmetrical and non-zero sum gains attendant to the policy (i.e., generally beneficial without any losers). In contrast, perceptions of NAFTA were almost completely the opposite. The domestic stakes were thought to be high (therefore, much more intermestic) and the prominence was also high (given that perceptions developed in particular about the asymmetrical and zero sum nature of the policy).

Gaining Control Over NAFTA and Its Expansion

One can argue that over the course of time, the passage of NAFTA shifted from the administrative model (low prominence, mainly international issue) to the political process model.

Perceptions of the domestic impact increased, fears about adverse and unequal results grew. As the intermestic character of NAFTA assumed greater importance, its prominence swelled. A quick check of news articles about NAFTA between 1980 and 1992 illustrate this rising attention paid to the treaty. In that twelve year span 358 articles were written about NAFTA. Of those 358 articles, 234 were written in 1992 only, accounting for 65% of the total. This clearly demonstrates the "spiking" interest about NAFTA which concentrated around the time of passage. Media coverage both reflected and added to public interest in NAFTA: it got media attention because of public concerns, yet at the same time, high media prominence fueled public fears. The number of actors involved in the passage increased dramatically; at the same time --and related to this growing number of participants-- certainty about passage decreased.

This experience taught a number of valuable lessons to those advocating NAFTA expansion. Three are particularly important: (1) silence (in terms of media coverage) is golden; (2) lower prominence is preferable; and (3) emphasize the international elements, minimize the intermestic impact. In addition to these lessons from the NAFTA experience, two other factors further encourage a deliberate policy of downplaying NAFTA: the 1996 Presidential campaign (no one wants it to be an issue, except those who oppose-- a minority of the presidential hopefuls); and the Mexican crisis, which calls into question the legitimacy and validity of the original NAFTA promises, thus --by extension-- compromising the reasoning behind NAFTA's expansion and the vision of the FTAA.

In order to avoid possible derailing of NAFTA's expansion, the government has developed a multiple strategy to overcome possible obstacles. In particular, the administration is working strenuously to prevent a shift to the political process model. The first move was the selection of Chile: a nation far away from the United States (less immigration threat), with a smaller economy (less competition). Overall, in comparison to Mexico, Chile is less "threatening" to domestic interests, therefore less likely to be caught in the "intermestic" trap as well as avoiding high prominence (since the situation lacks asymmetrical, zero sum perceptions).

Following the selection of Chile was deafening silence. There is really a type of official "quiet" about the accession process: little attention is given it by the Administration itself and the enlargement is proceeding under "SOP" tactics. Even the failure to attain "fast-track" status generated little attention: specifically, neither the Administration nor other supporters chose to make an issue of the bill.

What little is said about Chile tends to re-emphasize the symmetrical, non-zero sum benefits of expansion, as well as its more international components. For example, in a statement before the Subcommittees on the Western Hemisphere and on International Economic Policy and Trade of the House International Relations Committee (October 25, 1995), the Assistant Secretary for Inter-American Affairs focused on the benefits accruing to the United States from expansion. He stated bluntly that "[t]he U.S. has far more to gain than to lose from a mutual opening of markets in the hemisphere" [U.S. Department of State Dispatch: 803]. In addition, Assistant Secretary Watson signaled an international challenge that must be met by U.S. support for NAFTA expansion.

> Remember, too, that we are not the only actors in the drama. In addition to the momentum of sub-regional integration, Latin America is forming links outside the hemisphere, with the Asia-Pacific Economic Cooperation-APEC- and with the EU. ... Without U.S. leadership in structuring a liberalization process, the balance of interest and commitment in Latin America may well start to shift away from us [U.S. Department of State Dispatch: 803, emphasis added].

The latter part of the statement clearly raises traditional international concerns; as such, it tries to place the debate over NAFTA expansion into a more international rather than intermestic context.

An evaluation of accession proponents' strategy reveals mixed results. Using media coverage as one indication of prominence, it is evident that Chilean accession enjoys low rather than high prominence. A search of the InfoTrac database results in finding only 17 articles written about the Chilean accession since 1994 till the present. But, this lack of public prominence has not translated into greater control over the accession process. The best indication of this is the failure of fast-track bill. In essence, the "silent treatment" strategy has resulted in policy paralysis: in order to avoid attention, proponents of accession must avoid any substantial progress toward formal expansion.

Conclusion

The "disappearance" of NAFTA from official pronouncements and the invisibility of Chilean accession process makes sense in terms of models of foreign policy making. Proponents of expansion, wishing to gain control over the process, to lessen the number of actors involved and to avert a politicization of the process, are seeking first to minimize both the prominence of the issue as well as (to a lesser degree) emphasize its international character). Given the domestic context, these actions are understandable. However, they do give rise to some problems.

First, there is the question of "leadership" and the role it plays in policy-making. Does lessening the attention paid to an issue lead to passage of a controversial bill? Or, would allying the executive branch with the idea--in essence, White House (and other supporters) selling

NAFTA's extension be the key to passage? Many have argued that the key to the 1993 passage of NAFTA was the high profile given to the bill in the latter stages by the White House and others.

A second problem revolves around one of the other nation-state actors involved in the process. What is Chile suppose to do while U.S. proponents wait for an auspicious time to move toward accession? The silent strategy requires maximum flexibility: the government must be able to postpone decisions and/or actions until appropriate, inconspicuous times in the domestic arena. Can Chile put its plans on hold? Is it fair to ask another nation to shape its international policy around the domestic concerns of another nation?

The final dilemma associated with the U.S. strategy toward accession concerns the NAFTA partners and the question of foreign policy coordination. Coordination relies on standardized processes and procedures. The current strategy prevents the development of any type of regularized process of accession. In essence, it destroys the ability of Canada, Mexico and the United States to work together. Just as it asks Chile to put its plans on hold, so too does it demand maximum tolerance from partners.

Thus, this second year of NAFTA witnessed a loss of momentum toward regional integration. It suggests a negation of the Summit of the Americas and the plan for FTAA. More importantly, the United States actions imply that the country is not yet ready for any foreign policy agreement that requires coordination and cooperation across borders. The primacy of the domestic arena necessitates a loose connection between the United States and other nations.

Bibliography

Allison, Graham T. (1971). **The Essence of Decision: Explaining the Cuban Missile Crisis**. Boston, MA: Little, Brown.

Hilsman, Roger (1990). **The Politics of Policy Making in Defense and Foreign Affairs** (2nd Edition). Englewood Cliffs, NJ: Prentice Hall.

Rourke, John T., Ralph G. Carter and Mark A. Boyer (1994). **Making American Foreign Policy**. Guilford, CT: The Duskin Publishing Group, Inc.

Spanier, John W. And Eric M. Uslaner (1994). **American Foreign Policy Making and the Democratic Dilemmas** (6th Edition). New York, NY: Macmillan Publishing Company.

U.S. Department of State Dispatch (1995) "**The NAFTA Experience: Chile and the Future of Hemispheric Trade.**" Volume 6, No. 44, pgs. 803-804.

Whalen, Chris (1996). "**Mexico's Meltdown-Wait Till Next Year Amigo: Is Clinton Sending a Quiet Election Year Message to Bankrupt Mexico?**" The Washington Post, January 21, 1996, C3.

Wiarda, Howard J. (1990) **Foreign Policy Without Illusion.** Glenview, IL: Scott, Foresman.

Chapter IX

Clinton's New Foreign Policy Paradigm: An Analysis of U.S. Action Toward Haiti and Mexico

Alex Roberto Hybel

Introduction

Recent critics of the foreign policy of the United States have remarked that since the end of the Cold War Washington has functioned without a properly designed international compass, and that President Bill Clinton deserves much of the blame for this miscarriage. Some attribute the absence of direction in US foreign policy to his tendency to allow rhetorical devices to drive deeds, without first engaging in a judicious analysis of existing conditions and resources. One analyst suggests that "terms like "leadership," "credibility," "engagement," "sole remaining power," "moral ascendancy," and "American values" - have taken on a life of their own, a virtual reality that prompts policy decisions separate from any calculation of American interests."[1] Another analyst maintains that the failure to create a coherent foreign policy can be attributed to Clinton's inability to speak with "clarity and consistency about priorities and what the United States should be prepared to do on their behalf."[2]

In this paper I will argue that these criticisms are, for the most part, unfounded. I will assert that the end of the Cold War exposed not a hegemon incapable of designing a clear-minded foreign policy, but a state forced to acknowledge its democratic roots in a world that had become noticeably more uncertain and complex than it had been in nearly fifty years. I will also demonstrate that President Clinton, after a series of missteps, has been effective at creating a new foreign policy compass. I will postulate that Mr. Clinton, after realizing that his administration faced both a radically altered international system and a domestic system defined by a Congress determined to play a greater role in international affairs and a public reluctant to continue affording the costs of world hegemony, was successful at advancing his own foreign policy vision. I will support the argument with an analysis of President Clinton's decisions to intervene militarily in Haiti in September 1994, and to rescue Mexico's economy in early 1995.[3]

The Nature of the New Domestic Foreign Policy Environment

The November 1994 Congressional elections strengthened the conservative movement initiated in 1981 by President Ronald Reagan. The elections placed control of the Congress in the hands of a Republican Party determined to create a new foreign policy paradigm, restructure the nature and power of the federal government, and implant a new sense of fiscal responsibility. Its foreign policy agenda was driven by the belief that it was in the interest of the United States to promote an open market ideology and democracy, but constrained by the awareness that Americans cared little about developments in Somalia, Bosnia, Rwanda, Haiti, China or any Latin America country. It understood that most Americans were demanding that leaders make the internal problems of the United States their priority. As John. E. Rielly notes, "[s]elf interest has consistently dominated the public's assessment of foreign policy priorities over the past decade. But support for many of the humanitarian goals among both the public and leaders has declined to the lowest level in two decades. There has been a substantial decline in strong public support for protecting weaker countries against foreign aggression ..., for promoting and defending human rights in other countries ..., and for helping to improve the standard of living of less developed countries. A similar trend is evident among leaders."[4]

Clinton campaigned for the presidency convinced that foreign policy would not play a big role.[5] He was right. He defeated President George Bush, who had served as the first U.S. emissary to the People's Republic of China, as U.S. ambassador to the United Nations, as director of the Central Intelligence Agency, and as vice-president under Ronald Reagan before becoming president, and who had revealed his foreign policy adeptness during the invasion of Panama and the war against Iraq. To contend that Clinton was correct in his prediction is not to assert that he believed that foreign affairs would play a secondary role during his presidency.

Clinton's foreign policy has been pragmatic since its inception. As the first president to reach maturity during the Vietnam War, oppose it, and protest against it, he believes that it is in the interest of the United States to foster human rights, and to promote the creation and solidification of democratic regimes. He assumes that now that the United States no longer faces the threat of communism, there is no national interest "more urgent than securing democracy's triumph around the world."[6] This belief, however, has a solid pragmatic foundation. As his National Security Advisor Anthony Lake has noted, foreign policy must "marry principle and pragmatism. We should be principled about our purposes but pragmatic about our means."[7]

Clinton's pragmatic foundation has a second pillar. In a major speech at The American University, Clinton challenged the American public to ask itself whether it wanted to repeat the mistakes of the 1920s and 1930s by turning inward, or was ready to accept that the United States had become part of an interdependent world system. For the new president the choice was obvious. The American people, he noted, "are touched everywhere by the flows of commerce that cross national borders as inextricably as the weather ..."[8] Clinton is convinced that the American public must accept that the United States lives in a highly complex and interdependent world, and that any attempt to disregard this reality by turning inward would bring about very high costs.

In short, he advocates democratic regimes not because of their humanitarian value, but because they are more likely to foster market economies. The successor to a doctrine of containment, as Lake has noted, "must be a strategy of enlargement - enlargement of the world's free community of market democracies."[9] Does this mean that the United States will refuse to do business with a country that is undemocratic but is beginning to adhere to the tenets of the market economy, such as the People's Republic of China? Clearly not. Clinton's stand is no different from President Richard Nixon's, who found communism reprehensible and yet sought détente with its principal promoters.If détente was Nixon's modus operandi, the expansion of market-based economies is Clinton's central foreign policy strategy.

Haiti and Mexico

Messy situations effect untidy solutions. Few international cases corroborate this truism more forcefully than the Haitian case. President Clinton inherited the Haitian problem not from President George Bush, but from their predecessors all the way back to President Woodrow Wilson. President Wilson ordered the invasion of Haiti in July 1915, for fear that either Germany or France would try to establish a naval base in Haiti that would have threatened US control of the Windward Passage, the primary shipping route to the Panama Canal. Shortly after the invasion, Washington used the same strategy it had employed at the beginning of the century against Cuba to ensure that its new constitution would not undermine the interests of the United States on the island.[10] After placing Haiti's military, police force, and treasury under the control of the United States, Washington forced Haiti to ratify a constitution drafted by the U.S. Department of State and to agree to a 20-year US-Haiti treaty. "U.S. reforms had few lasting effects of any kind, good or bad, for 19 years was too short a time; goals were unclear and inconsistent except for ensuring that no other power would intervene; linguistic differences and racial prejudice limited communication; no significant, sustained, externally financed aid program was tried; and US techniques of rule contradicted expressed US desires for stability, respect for law, and institutionalization."[11]

In 1945, just 11 years after U.S. troops had left Haiti, the Haitian military overthrew President Elie Lescot who, upon reaching the end of his term of office, had tried to change the constitution so that he could succeed himself. Five years later, the military intervened again to overthrow Lescot's successor, Dumarsais Estimé. In 1956, Estimé's successor, Paul Magliore, experienced the same fate. It was not until 1957, when Dr. François Duvalier was elected president, that the rash of military coups in Haiti came to a halt. The end of this trend, however, did not mark the beginning of a better era. Duvalier consolidated his power, as no one else had ever done, by destroying the military as an independent force, creating additional lines of communication with the rural world, expelling the foreign clergy, and politicizing the educational system.[12] Duvalier was succeeded by his son, Jean-Claude, in 1971. The new Duvalier, who managed to remain in power until 1986, did nothing to slow down the process of deterioration that had plagued Haiti since the departure of the United States in 1934. Political and economic conditions worsened so badly that in 1984 the inhabitants of Raboteau, a slum in the regional city of Gonaïves, revolted against the government. More demonstrations followed, and in January 1986, the leadership of the army ordered the troops not to shoot at the civilian population. A month later, President Reagan's Secretary of State George Schultz made it clear during a television interview that Jean-Claude would have to go. Duvalier, realizing that he no longer had the support of the United States or the Haitian army, left the country on February 7. His departure was followed by a series of costly missteps. The elections held in November 1987 were stopped by the army after a few hours of voting; the ones held in January 1988 secured the participation of only 5% of the population and the elected government was overthrown in June of the same year; the military government that came to power in June was expelled in September by non-commissioned officers; and the president of the new regime lasted until March 1990, when he was forced to resign after failing to organize fair democratic elections. New elections were held in December 1990, at which time Father Jean-Bertrand Aristide, a political activist, was elected. He assumed power in January 1991 but was overthrown in September of the same year.[13] The overthrow of President Aristide forced the United States to stop pretending that Haiti was not its problem.

Criticism of the decision by the Clinton administration to intervene in Haiti's domestic affairs has been deficient on several counts. First, failure on the part of the Clinton administration to intervene would have undermined the reputation of the United States in the region. Though the death of communism did not bring about the demise of international military threats, it helped alter the definition of the national interest.[14] The threat of nuclear war has been replaced by the reality of a social bomb smoldering in our midst. It is not enough to speak of state security. Security of the nation-state and its borders defended by stockpiles of weapons and exclusive economic development is no longer sufficient. Human security, that is the security of communities, of individuals and their basic needs and freedoms, has become a primary component of the national interest.[15] As acknowledged by Congressman Richard J. Durbin of Illinois, it is in the best interest of the United States "to see stability and progress in Haiti ... Democracy in Haiti and the surrounding nations not only sets a good example, but is what America has always been about... [T]he illegal immigration from Haiti was creating problems which ... were unbearable, not only for the State of Florida but for many other States. As long as the political and economic instability continued in Haiti, more illegal immigrants would risk their lives to come to our shores. It is part of the national interest of the United States to make certain that illegal immigration is at least diminished if not stopped."[16] A consortium of Latin American states had sought to bring about a solution to the Haitian problem to no avail, and it was only when the Clinton administration decided to act aggressively that a glimmer of hope surfaced. This is not to say that it will succeed, but even if it fails the other parties will know that the region's hegemon was willing to pay the cost of failure.

Second, to suggest that the Clinton administration was inconsistent for intervening in Haiti but not in Rwanda, Sudan, China, and Syria, where human rights were are also being violated, is to concede that the president and his advisers were realistic about the ability of the United States to influence events. The concept of national interest cannot be employed as a utility function in rigorous policy analysis. It encompasses a variety of subgoals that compete for influence in the conduct of foreign policy. The relative weight given to subgoals is a "matter left to the authoritative (but subjective) judgment of top-level officials."[17] As Anthony Lake has noted, the United States should "help foster and consolidate democracies and market economies, **where possible, especially in states of special significance and opportunity**."[18] President Clinton seconded Lake's statement in his 1996 State of the Union speech when he stated: "We can't go everywhere. We can't do everything. But where our interests and our values are at stake - and where we can make a difference - America must lead."[19]

Third, to contend that the Clinton administration failed to design a coherent foreign policy toward Haiti is to disregard that its foreign policy was defined as much by the incertitude that emanated from Haiti as by the uncertainty that flowed from the domestic domain.[20] On June 16, 1993, after extensive lobbying by the Clinton administration, the UN Security Council authorized a worldwide oil and arms embargo against Haiti, along with an assets freeze. Failure of this action to force the Haitian military government to reinstate Aristide as president forced the UN to approve an almost complete economic embargo of Haiti on May 6, 1994. On June 10, a month after the Haitian military had announced that Supreme Court Judge Emile Jonassaint had been named provisional president, the Clinton administration announced it would cut off US commercial flights to Haiti, and tightened other sanctions. At the end of July, the UN Security Council authorized by a vote of 12 to 0 the use of force against Haiti. On September 16, a day after issuing a blunt warning to Haiti's military leaders that their time was "up - leave now or we'll force you from power," Clinton dispatched to Haiti former President Jimmy Carter, former Joint Chiefs of Staff Chairman General Colin L. Powell, and Senate Armed Services Committee Chairman Sam Nunn to try to persuade the nation's military leaders to step down voluntarily. The blue-ribbon panel persuaded

Haiti's military leaders to authorize the arrival of US troops on September 19, and to cede power to President Aristide on October 15. This entire process took place in a U.S. domestic environment unwilling to support any form of U.S. military action against Haiti. A poll conducted in early July 1994 recorded that 68 percent of those surveyed opposed an invasion, while only 23 percent favored it. By September 12, when it became evident that Clinton would authorize an invasion, the majority of members of Congress opposed it.

Finally, to purport that failure by earlier administrations to change Haiti's domestic structure should have informed the Clinton administration that it could not succeed, is to disregard the facts that the United States had never attempted to build democracy in Haiti, that present conditions in the international arena are more conducive to the formation of democratic regimes than they were in the past, and that Washington is not the sole party responsible for the task. It is still too early to determine whether Haiti will build a stable democratic structure and a sound economic system. But it is not too early to contend that those who predicted that Aristide would not relinquish power at the end of his presidential term and would then turn against the United States, and that the United States would become bogged down in Haiti with no clear exit strategy, were wrong.[21]

On December 19, 1994, exactly three months after US troops had landed on Haiti, the Clinton administration found itself facing a new, but very different, foreign policy crisis. On that date, Mexico devalued the peso, which had been pegged at 3.5 to the dollar. By then, dollar reserves in Mexico had shrunk to $11 billion, which was not enough to pay dollar-pegged bonds that were about to be due shortly. More money left the country, bringing the reserves down to $5 billion, thus forcing the government to announce that it could no longer guarantee dollars for pesos at any price. This announcement forced the peso to fall dramatically and stocks to tumble.These developments took a great number of people by surprise.[22] Mexico's economy had changed markedly for the better since 1982, when the government ran a deficit equal to 16% of GDP and had defaulted on millions of dollars in loan payments. By 1994, Mexico had balanced its budget three years in a row, sold costly state-owned companies, and appropriated an open-market policy by becoming part of the North American Free Trade Agreement (NAFTA). These attractive economic features, however, were enfeebled by the fact that Mexico borrowed and bought too much from the international market, but sold too little, thus driving the current-account deficit to more than $28 billion, which was the equivalent of 8% of the country's GDP. In the words of Stanley Fischer, a deputy managing director with the International Monetary

Fund, Mexico did "everything right - with one exception, and you can't do that thing wrong."[23]

The Clinton administration came to Mexico's rescue in a relatively short period of time. Mexico's Finance Minister Guillermo Ortiz traveled to Wall Street and Washington in early January 1995 with a plan to revamp Mexico's economy and bring back foreign capital. After explaining that Mexico's government was ready to cut spending and that the labor unions would hold wage gains to 7%, Ortiz was able to get an $18 billion credit line from international leaders, and an augmentation of the credit line in loan guarantees from President Clinton. On January 12, Clinton proposed a $40 billion Mexican aid package to the US Congress. To ensure proper repayment of the loan, his administration stipulated that Mexico pay substantial fees up front to more than cover scoring costs, provide backing in the form of proceeds from exports in the event it could not meet its obligations, and agree to new strict monetary and fiscal policies designed to restore growth and thereby generate resources to repay its obligations. It also demanded that Mexico undertake further structural changes, including further privatization steps.

On January 23, Secretary of Treasury Robert Rubin and Federal Reserve Chairman Alan Greenspan went to Congress to ask support for Clinton's plan. The following day, Clinton, in his State of the Union address, stated that it was in the interest of the United States to help Mexico resolve the economic crisis. Initially, it seemed that their plea would fall on receptive ears. Speaker of the House Newt Gingrich stated that the Republicans in Congress had "zero choice" but to approve Clinton's request. Senator Robert Dole, the Senate Majority Leader, agreed with Gingrich. But in short time it became evident that the new Republican Congress was not about to give up the chance to embarrass the White House. On January 27, Gingrich announced that the Congress would not support Clinton's plan. Four days later, Clinton bypassed the Congress and used the Exchange Stabilization Fund to authorize $20 billion in loans and loan guarantees to Mexico.

Clinton's action instigated several rebukes from members of Congress. Senator Jesse Helms, chairman of the Senate Foreign Relations Committee, accused Clinton of violating the "will of the American people," argued that the bailout would be "unfair to American taxpayers," speculated that the scheme would do "nothing to remedy Mexico's internal problems," and maintained that failure to implement it would not result in the disaster suggested by the Clinton administration. Senator Lauch Faircloth added fuel to the fire by stating that he firmly believed that the loans to Mexico would never be repaid.

Critics of Clinton's decision were either indifferent to or ignorant of the effect that failure on the part of Washington to try to help rescue Mexico's economy would have on the interests of the United States. It is still unclear whether Mexico's economy will rebound. In early August 1995, there were some promising signs. The government had managed to meet its obligations to holders of $1.2 billion of tesobonos, thus bringing to a successful close the most testing month of tesobono repayment, and leaving only some $6 billion outstanding, down from $22 billion in early 1995; the stock market had rallied; and exports during the first six months of 1995 were 32% higher than during the first half of 1994. In fact, at that time it was suggested that Mexico might be experiencing a recovery similar to Turkey's.[24] Three months later, however, the Mexican peso dropped 26% against the US dollar, inflation was running at 50%, and the GDP was expected to decline 5%. But to propound that it is too early to predict whether Mexico's economy will bounce back, is not to suggest that Clinton should not have extended an assisting hand.

Clinton knew that he did not have a choice. He became president convinced that the economic well-being of the United States is tightly linked to the steady expansion of market-based economies. The vision is not novel, but for some forty years it had been blurred by the perceived need to contain communism. The demise of communism brought the competition for a national interest modus operandi to an end — the promotion of market-based economies became the central tenet.

The decision by Clinton to assist Mexico was defined by three tightly linked national interest considerations. First, he, and especially Secretary of State Warren Christopher, understood that leadership exerts a decisive influence upon national power, and that leadership is linked to a policy of prestige designed to "impress other nations with the power one's own nation actually possesses, or with the power it believes, or wants other nations to believe, it possesses."[25] Christopher acknowledged this much when he stated that the decision to help Mexico was, probably more than anything else, "a test of American leadership. By extending this package to Mexico, the United States will demonstrate its unwavering commitment to lead this hemisphere toward stability and prosperity... Only the United States has the capacity to offer this leadership." Also implied in the statement, but clarified in another portion of his testimony, was the notion that if the United States hoped to protect the essential rules governing interstate economic relations, it had to protect its weaker partners. The United States provides this service because it recognizes that its own welfare is tightly linked to the welfare of the international regime it dominates.

The approval of the loan guarantee package, stated Christopher, would "have far-reaching implications for the prosperity and stability of Latin America and of emerging market economies around the world." The third and final consideration referred to by the Clinton administration centered on the economic and political interconnection between Mexico and the United States. One need not be a Marxist to know that one of the primary objectives of the dominant capitalist state is to maintain macroeconomic prosperity for the capitalist system. The state's primary role is "to create and maintain structural conditions in the global economic system that will prove conducive to the protection and expansion of the domestic political system."[26] The United States, explained Christopher, "has an immense economic and political stake in Mexico's stability... If we fail to act decisively now, American investment to Mexico will be imperiled. American export — now $40 billion a year — will diminish. And many of the 700,000 American jobs those exports support could be jeopardized ... [E]conomic distress and political instability in Mexico could add to the pressure that already pushes thousands of illegal immigrants across the 2,000-mile border that we share ... Moreover, Mexico's capacity to cooperate with us on a range of other issues — from narcotics trafficking and money laundering to the environment — could be severely strained."[27]

A New Foreign Policy Paradigm

It may seem premature to propose that the United States has finally settled on a foreign policy paradigm, considering that the international system has yet to reveal fully its structures and that in 1997 the United States may be led by a new president. It is not. The foundations of the new paradigm have been in place for quite some time. The difference between now and fifty years ago is that for the first time since at least 1945 the foreign policy paradigm of the United States is being defined by a single modus operandi — the creation, protection, and enlargement of market democracies. This objective is not sought indiscriminately. As Anthony Lake has noted, the United States cannot allow "this overarching goal to drive us into overarching actions. To be successful, a strategy of enlargement must provide distinctions and priorities."[28] The actions by the Clinton administration toward Haiti and Mexico support this claim and it is unlikely that any new U.S president would reject the new paradigm in the near future.

Notes

1 Jonathan Clarke, "Rhetoric Before Reality," Foreign Affairs, Vol. 74, No. 2, Sep./Oct. 1995: 3.
2 Richard Haas, "Paradigm Lost," Foreign Affairs, Vol. 74, No. 1, Jan./Feb/1995: 45.
3 President Clinton's decision regarding Bosnia would also be an important case study, but since this paper focuses on the foreign policy of the United States toward Latin America, such a case will not be studied.
4 See John E. Rielly, "The Public Mood at Mid-Decade," in Foreign Policy, Spring 1995, No. 98: 81.
5 See Bob Woodward, The Agenda. NY: Simon and Schuster, 1994: 22.
6 Quoted in Tony Smith, "In Defense of Intervention," Foreign Affairs, Vol. 73, No. 6: 40.
7 Anthony Lake, "From Containment to Enlargement," Johns Hopkins University, School of Advanced International Studies, Sept. 21, 1993: 14.
8 Quoted in Haynes Johnson, Divided We Fall. NY: W.W. Norton and Company, 1994: 39.
9 Lake, 1993: 5.
10 I am referring to the Platt Amendment, which was accepted by the Cuban Constitutional Convention by a vote of 15 to 11 in 1901. As the top US military commander in Cuba, General Leonard Wood, acknowledged in a letter to Theodore Roosevelt, the amendment left little or no independence to Cuba. Walter LaFeber, The American Age. NY.: W.W. Norton, 1989: 197.
11 Brian Weinstein and Aaron Segal, Haiti: The Failure of Politics. NY.: Praeger, 1992: 32.
12 Ibid.: 39-42.
13 Michele S. Laguerre, The Military and Society in Haiti. Knoxville, TN: The University of Tennessee Press, 1993: 3-4.
14 This contention, however, is not acknowledged by everybody. Senator Robert Dole, for instance, claims that "Haiti poses no strategic threat to theUnited States," and argues that if "human rights violations were enough rea son for United States intervention, we would be invading most countries in the world - Rwanda, Sudan, China, Syria, and many more."
15 "The Search for Human Security: Main Political Challenge for the UN," Speech delivered by Ambassador Juan Somavia at the Global Welfare 94 International Conference of ICSW, in Tampere, Finland, May 16, 1994.
16 House of Representatives Congressional Record, October 6, 1994: H11059.
17 Alexander L. George and Robert O. Keohane, "The Concept of National Interests: Uses and Limitations," in Alexander L. George, Presidential Decisionmaking in Foreign Policy: The Effective Use of Information and

Advice. Boulder: Westview Press, 1980: 219.

18 Lake, 1993: 6. My emphasis.

19 William Clinton, "State of the Union Speech: We Must Go Forward," The New York Times, Jan. 24, 1996: 14.

20 This challenge also disregards the fact that previous administrations had used in other cases a wide range of diplomatic measures, along with economic sanctions and threats of force, with few positive results.

21 For an account of Congressional opposition to Clinton's Haitian policy, see Carroll J. Doherty, "President, Rebuffing Congress, Prepares to Launch Invasion," Congressional Quarterly, Sep. 17, 1994: 2578-83.

22 I am not suggesting that everybody was caught by surprise. The IMF presumably warned Mexican officials privately that the country's current-account problem could cause problems, but chose not to go public for fear hat it would instigate a run on the peso. See Lee Smith, "Time To Buy Mexico?" Fortune, Feb. 6, 1995: 124.

23 Smith, Feb. 6, 1995: 123.

24 Turkey got into trouble due to a rapidly increasing current-account deficit in January 1994, but after a year and a half, its economy was growing again, the current-account deficit had disappeared, and the stockmarket was rising so strongly that it had become one of the world's top perfor mers. The Economist, August 5, 1995: 68-9.

25 Hans Morgenthau, Politics Among Nations. NY: Knopf, 1985: 87.

26 Alex Roberto Hybel, How Leaders Reason. Oxford: Basil Blackwell, 1990: 21.

27 Warren Christopher, Statement Before the House Committee on Banking, Finance and Urban Affairs, U.S. Department of State, Office of the Spokesman, January 25, 1995.

28 Lake, 1993: 5.

Chapter X

NAFTA's Foreign Policy Coordination: The Cuban Test

David R. Dávila - Villers *

"Yes. The United States will be here 200 years and it can continue to shoot men for that little space until they learn to vote and rule themselves."[2]

Summary: Mexico, Canada and Europe have cordial diplomatic relations with Cuba; but the US continues its fading blockade on the island. This paper is an exploration of the Cuban "isolation" and its implications for the NAFTA's foreign policy coordination.

The Cuban Revolution and its meaning for North America

The Cuban Revolution is probably the single most important event affecting the inter-American relations during the XX century, the most compelling reason for this being the fact of introducing superpower competition in the hemisphere. It may be asserted however, that neither Canada nor Mexico shared the US particular views regarding the Cuban process. Accordingly, the Cuban revolution was differently perceived in the three North American countries. This is especially true of hegemonic US and post-revolutionary Mexico.

* Profesor of International Relations and History at the Universidad de las Américas-Puebla.

With the benefit of time, academic interpretations of such revolutionary process seem to coincide in several respects. Two are crucial to understand Cuba:

1. The original course of the Cuban revolution was not Socialist. It was rather the lack of options that led a young and pragmatic leadership to opt for the Socialist bloc.[3] The same pragmatism is leading Fidel Castro to seek for survival alternatives after the collapse of the Soviet Union.

2. The US foreign policy toward the island pushed the young Cuban revolution into the arms of the Soviets. Nowadays, the US foreign policy is pushing Cuba away, once more, into non-hemispheric arms.

The Cuban revolution for the US

In the midst of superpower competition, the emergent Cuban revolution spelt disaster for the US. The prevalent opinion was "the Russians are at our doorstep". And after having sympathized with Fidel Castro (several of the main pro-Castrite support committees were originally based in the US), the US endeavored to isolate the Cuban regime, to sabotage and blockade the Cuban economy, to assassinate Fidel Castro,[4] and to invade the island[5].

This aggressive US attitude convinced the Cuban leadership that there was no other way out but the Soviets. Neither the Europeans, nor the Japanese or the Chinese were able and willing to come to Fidel's rescue, as these three world powers were in the making during the 60's.

Thus, Cuba deepened its statisation process, becoming the first Socialist country in the Western Hemisphere, to the great chagrin of a quite large list of successive US administrations. In time, the Cuban revolution would inspire and support liberation movements in Latin America, the Caribbean, even Africa; which could only confirm US policy-makers in their beliefs about the Castro regime. Nothing, short of Fidel's overthrow, would satisfy them. A large Cuban emigration to Miami would provide them with the support needed: a powerful and conservative anti-Havana lobby in Washington.

The Cuban revolution for Mexico

Far from sharing the US perspective, Mexico's view of the Cuban process was (and is) quite different, as could be expected from a populist Latin American regime. Mexico has always had friendly relations with Socialist Cuba, against the desires of its powerful northern neighbor. Fidel Castro was actually exiled in Mexico from 1953 to 1955, after his first (failed) assault to the Moncada quarters.[6] Castro prepared his expeditionary troop in Mexico, the Granma actually sailed to Cuba from the Veracruz coast, and there seems to be no hard evidence that the Mexican government had repressed Castro's guerrilla.

After the economic blockade was imposed on the island, the US would try and coerce most of its hemispheric "allies" to adopt a similar standing. The Mexican diplomacy, like the other Latin American countries', was subjected to severe strain, but it did not yield to US pressure to break relations with Cuba. Not even if the US president called personally his Mexican similar, Adolfo López Mateos. General Lázaro Cárdenas and his followers (the National Liberation Movement), mounted a national campaign to support the Cubans. Cárdenas even volunteered to fight for Cuba but was prevented by a cautious López Mateos.

In July 1964, when the OAS voted diplomatic sanctions against the island, Mexico rejected the resolution and maintained its diplomatic ties and airline connection with Cuba. Mexico even increased the amount of its investment in the island (from US $922 million in 1959 to US$ 1 300 in 1964). [7]

To be fair, other Latin American countries also refused to break diplomatic relations with Cuba before 1964. But also during the 60's, with the exception of Venezuela, Costa Rica and Mexico, all the Latin American countries fell prey to military dictatorships. The US government, it is worth not to forget, maintained cordial diplomatic relations with all those authoritarian regimes that exiled, jailed, tortured and killed thousands of men, women and children.[8] All those authoritarian regimes were allies to the US in a Saint Crusade against Communism.

Mexico, on the other hand, severed relations with the dictators (the case of Pinochet being the most studied) and offered asylum to thousands of Latin Americans. Cuba did the same. And so it was, from the middle of the 60's to the beginning of the 80's. After their return to civilian rule, all Latin American countries have re-established diplomatic relations with Havana.

The Cuban revolution for Canada

In strong contrast with Mexico and the US, Canada was not effected by the Cuban events. No considerable impact, if at all, is mentioned in major accounts of Canadian history. Canada was not in control of its government, yet. For the record, however, it is important to note that neither Britain, nor Canada broke relations with Cuba. Quite the contrary, Canadian trade whith the island expanded during this period. As we will see later on, Canada is currently one of the main investors in the island and one of the main enemies of the Helms-Burton legislation.

King Sugar and the longevity of the Castro regime

The Cuban economy is a clear example of the flaws of mono-production. Sugar has remained the king crop under the Spaniards, the Americans and the Russians. Mono-production, however, should not be mistaken for pre-capitalism. Quite the contrary, the confrontation between the US and the Cuban revolution was a direct consequence of highly capitalized and monopolized sugar production.

"King Sugar" —Eduardo Galeano[9] dixit— is to blame for the over-concentration of private ownership that led to the unbearable situation where most Cubans labored for the foreign owners (mainly US citizens) of the "national" capital. Therefore, for the Cubans, the agrarian reform implied direct confrontation with the US.

Soon after seizing power, the Castroites too will find impossible to change the only industry that could secure a national income. . . and so Cuba went on (as Nicolás Guillén would have it) firing "sugar-sugar bullets" that the Soviets used to buy at US 40.78 cents a pound (while it rated 7.80 only, in the international markets). At the same time, the USSR and the Eastern Bloc supplied Cuba of almost everything. It is said that the USSR should have financed an estimate of 15% to 20% of the Cuban "global social product" (i.e.: 150 billion US dollars in 30 years, plus a billion and a half of military assistance, every year). Subsidized development? Indeed.[10] But Cuba looked splendid! Those were the golden years of Socialism. Most of the Cubans enjoyed impressive social welfare benefits: education, food, health care, housing, etc., while the rest of Latin America went through a seemingly unending night of military dictatorships.

The Cuban experience was perceived by many Latin Americans as a good option to marginality, poverty, unemployment, repression and massive Human Rights violations under the military governments.

The collapse of the Eastern Bloc and the subsequent Cuban crisis has made the island to turn its eyes to tourism as a source of income, and to foreign investment.[11] Once more, development comes from abroad. Cuba is looking for another power that could replace the USSR. . . Spain,[12] Canada and Italy are among the most important investors and trade partners of the island. Canada matters more for the author of this paper than the other two Cuban partners. We are talking of a 300 million US dollars worth trade[13] between the two countries. Canada supplies Cuba with North American products, and Cuba sells its sugar in the Canadian market.

Several indicators point to an economic recovery of Cuba. Since 1994, Cuba started growing again, after four years of negative rates (1989-1993). The Real GDP shows a positive number since 1994.[14] There has been a reduction in the government deficit. Imports and exports have slightly recovered. Sugar and manioc prices are down (since the production was liberalized). The dollar rate in the black market is also down. Dollar remittances from the US are still arriving through Mexico, Venezuela and Canada, in spite of the US government prohibition. In all, however, the state of the Cuban economy is still delicate. For 1996, the Cuban government estimated a 5% GDP growth and a sugar production of 4.4 million tons.

On the political side, the desires (should I say the dreams?) of many US administrations from Kennedy to Clinton shall remain unfulfilled: The Cuban government is not collapsing, and the US foreign policy towards Cuba is, in part, to blame. Fidel Castro is no Ceausescu, and his popularity is unrivaled in Cuba, thanks —I dare say— to the US ! Populist charismatic leaders like Castro (or Saddam Hussein, for the matter) will be indispensable, to the eyes of their peoples, for as long as the US continues to aggress their countries. In such circumstances, strong governments are the only alternative left. Furthermore, the US is dealing with a government that is promoting change, a government that retains a great capacity for adaptation to new international circumstances. Fidel and his followers are leading the Cuban transition towards a mixed economy and will continue to be the leaders of such a change. It is a desirable change, and of course, Cuba is more likely to make democratic progresses and to complete its transition towards a mixed economy if the US lifts the embargo.

The Helms-Burton and the European Community

Let us talk now about the "diplomatic war" between Cuba and the US, which is another war that the US is poised to lose. Latin America is in favor of Cuba's return to the Organization of American States. And the subcontinent is not alone in this. On 16th July 1993, at the end of the Ibero-American Summit, all Latin American countries plus Spain and Portugal (with the notorious exception of Ménem) demanded the lift of the embargo. And on 24th March 1994, in Lima, the OAS Secretary General, João Baena Suárez, re-iterated his support to Cuba's return to the Organization. Four times, the issue of the US blockade over the island has been brought to vote in the UN, and four times the UN has condemned the US stance towards Cuba.[15] The Helms-Burton initiative (see chronology at the end of this paper) has provoked similar reactions from the international community. On 23 May 1995, the Group of Río condemned the extra-territorial application of the law as unacceptable, at a request from Mexico. On 18 October 1995, nineteen heads of state of Latin America plus Spain and Portugal rejected the blockade against the island and severely criticized the Helms-Burton inititive as a unilateral coercive measure that violates states' sovereignty and international law. Furthermore, on 5 March 1996, the Canadian Prime Minister plus the heads of the fourteen CARICOM states also rejected the law. The EU is challenging the Helms-Burton law in the World Trade Organization. Finally, Canada and Mexico decided to join forces to fight against the law, in the framework of the NAFTA.

The Cuban exile in the US is no longer monolithic (if it ever was). Two of the three main organizations of the Cuban exile in the US, with a superior combined force than Más Canosa's *Fundación Nacional Cubano-Americana*, are favorable to the re-establishment of diplomatic relations with Cuba. Those organizations, formed in 1993, are *Cambio Cubano* and the *Comité Cubano por la Democracia.*[16]

On 24th February 1996, two civilian airplanes from the US were shot down by the Cuban Air Force. The crew of four *Hermanos al Rescate* (a Cuban exile organization) was killed. The incident caused the interruption of the dialogue between the European Community and Cuba leading to a possible cooperation agreement. The EU had also important reservations regarding democracy in the island which the Cuban government was not ready to concede.

However, the Cuban economy has indeed went through important reforms that had benefited the Europeans. In 1989, the EU represented 6% of the total Cuban foreign trade. By 1994, 38% of the Cuban exports and 29% of its imports were traded with Europe. Nearly half of the 230 "mixed industries" function with European capital. EU economic and humanitarian assistance increased from 6 million Ecu in 1993 to 15 in 1995.[17]

On its side, the Clinton Administration intends to tighten the embargo against Cuba by enforcing the Helms-Burton Law. In theory, this measure would affect (besides Canadian and Mexican companies) no less than 100 European firms; i.e.: *Grupo Sol* and *Argentaria* form Spain, *Benetton* and *STET* from Italy, *Pernod/Ricard* from *France, Tate & Lyle* from the U.K. and *Mercedes Benz* from Germany.

The president of the European Community, Mr. Jacques Santer warned president Clinton that the EU would apply counter-sanctions against the US if European companies were affected by the Helms-Burton Law. EU counter-measures would include: trade restrictions to US products, freezing of funds, and the erection of a WTO tribunal to face the US sanctions against European companies. Mr. Santer also stated that EU, as the US, wants to promote democracy and human rights in the island, but such objective —Mr. Santer said— is nct going to be reached through economic sanctions. [18]

A similar position was assumed by the Canadian government. On June 14th, the Minister of Foreign Affairs, Lloyd Axworthy and the Minister of International Trade, Art Eggleton announced that the government had decided to take provisions against the Helms-Burton Law, including counter-sanctions.[19] At the same time, and in coordination with Mexico, Canada has maintained consultations in the framework of the NAFTA. A panel for the solution of this controversy could be created 30 days after the three ministers of foreign trade convene at a Commission session.[20]

Art Eggleton affirmed that the Helms-Burton Law runs against the international legal principles. Canada, as the US, wants better human rights standards and a more representative government in Cuba —the Minister said—but the Helms-Burton Law is taking the wrong approach.[21]

Mexico, whose own proclaimed foreign policy principle of *non-intervention* prevents it from "qualifying" the representativity of the Cuban regime, is preparing an "antidote law" (as might the rest of Latin American countries) to protect Mexican companies from the extra-territorial application of the Helms-Burton Law. Cuba, on its side, has prepared a new legislation to claim up to 65 billion from the US due to 34 years of illegal blockade. The US, not cuba, has become an island (in diplomatic terms)!

I would like to repeat my point once more: Cuba is more likely to make democratic progresses and to complete its transition towards a mixed economy if the US lifts the embargo. But, of course, we will have to wait until the next US president finally realize that the US foreign policy is fundamentally wrong.

Allowing Cuba to set yet another example to the Third World

The US foreign policy has served an unintended purpose for sure. It does have allowed Cuba to set yet another example to the Third World. The example of a poor country fit to survive the US anachronistic aggression, a country that, in the middle of its worst crisis ever, maintains (unlike most of the Americas) its national health service and its national educational system.

This is no little thing at all if we consider the effect Neoliberal policies have brought about to Latin Americans. Some of the "economies" (term that strangely enough seem to exclude the peoples) of the region have "progressed"; but unemployment, poverty, etc., not to speak about the return of almost forgotten diseases, have increased with a vengeance.

Neoliberalism is on the spot. Even the Pope is giving us a *holly helping hand* to exhibit the misery of an approach that purports the "free competition" between the opulent and the miserable. With very limited resources, and unlike many other countries, Cuba continues to invest in its people. In that sense, Cuba is again setting an example worth following. But its polity has still to go through a democratization process.

I want to insist once more in that a populist charismatic leader like Castro will be indispensable, to the eyes of his people, for as long as the US continues to aggress the country. Surely the lesson to be learned from what has happened until now is that the Cuban establishment is likely to survive. A young new generation of Socialist Cubans (like Chancelor Robaina) is ready to accept the relay.

Cuba: between the EU and the NAFTA

It is now time to discuss the alternatives offered to the US government if, besides Europe, Canada and Mexico sustain and even develop closer relations with Cuba. Because while it is true, on the one hand, that the NAFTA is not about foreign policy coordination, the other side of the coin is that North American integration is heavy in foreign policy implications.

According to Cuban sources, Canada has become the number one foreign investor already (nickel, oil, etc.), ahead of Spain (tourism). As far as Mexico (cellular telephones) is concerned, we speculate that Carlos Salinas de Gortari is one of the main individual investors with the "little savings" he made when he was president of Mexico.[22] Clearly, the US enforced blockade of the island runs at the encounter of the economic interests of the two other NAFTA countries, which have considerably invested in the Cuban economy. It can be said that the Helms-Burton law is the US reaction to the economic recovery of Cuba in the post-Soviet era; it is an angry reaction to the Cuban success in attracting foreign partnership.

A few years ago, the joke was: "China is a country without a market, Japan is a market without a country, and the European Community is a supermarket without a manager." Since then, however, the "supermarket" has become the largest one in the world, including 15 countries; concentrating, at the same time, the world largest GDP.

Its financial strength is evident.[23] The EU is currently deciding the terms of a new currency that shall substitute all national currencies in Europe: the "Euro".[24] The French nuclear tests have not gone unnoticed to anybody —I hope— or the European efforts towards a single European army. So the joke is not laughing matter anymore !

The EU has a common market, a common agricultural policy, a single space program, etc. Paradoxical though it may seem, and in spite of all this combined force, the EU has no common foreign policy (is the Helms-Burton law auspiciating a first rehearsal?). Without this and a powerful army, the EU will continue to be a group of very important lesser powers.

The EU exists economically and that should be enough for Cuba. Miguel Marín, the Spaniard vice-president of the European Commission and Isabel Allende, the Cuban vice-chancellor have been recently discussing the terms of a cooperation agreement, that was interrupted (not cancelled) by the Hermanos al Rescate affair, as we have seen.[25]

This brings us to the Association of Caribbean States, including the Group of Three (Colombia, Venezuela and Mexico), the CARICOM (fourteen West Indian countries) and Cuba. Set aside the anti-embargo impact, the inclusion in this association allows the country to establish direct links with the EU area of influence, ruled by the Lomé Convention. Thus Cuba is not only breaking the embargo at the regional level, it may also be allowed to assume the role of a "big" country in the European-influenced Caribbean region. Clearly, the US-enforced blockade of the island goes against European Union interests, as well. In other terms, what the US is doing is to break the unity of the NAFTA while it faces a quite cohesive EU at the same time !

NAFTA Foreign Policy Coordination

The enactment of the NAFTA was certainly a good step towards regulating the asymmetric complex interdependence that characterizes the northern part of this hemisphere. Unquestionably, the idea behind the creation of such free trade area is to enhance North American competitiveness vis-à-vis the other main trading blocs; but arguably enough, the United States does not seem ready to adapt to the changes it entails, nor it seems ready to cop with the spill-over effects.[26]

A North American economy (out of the Canadian, Mexican and the US economies) already exists, but unlike the European case, there is a visible lack of an institution that could effectively coordinate a common North American foreign economic policy, and that despite the NAFTA being an economic agreement only. The fact of the matter is that integration among North American countries has gone beyond the framework of an agreement conceived as only economic, and the US is failing to provide the much needed leadership for the advancement of the NAFTA. Such a lack of US leadership is the more deeply felt because the North American region is not living its best moment in political terms either. Quite the contrary, the US foreign policy towards Cuba and the enactment of the Helms-Burton Law might well be the occasion of serious discord among NAFTA countries.

Besides the economic reasons so far explored, the three governments have been using the Cuban affair for "external extraction" purposes. Canada's national unity is at stake, with the Quebec affair. Canada is in need of foreign policy objectives that are shared by both Anglo and French Canadians, objectives that could unify the country: it is a matter of national unity. Mexico suffers one of its worst economic and political crises ever, and the Mexican government has repeatedly used its support for Cuba to rally support in times of hardship. So is Mexico doing, and for the above mentioned reasons, as well: it is a matter of national stability. The Clinton administration facing an election year went as far as to promise the end of the Castro regime in exchange for votes: it is a matter of permanence in power.

In the present context, however, the lack of a North American foreign policy coordination can have disastrous consequences for the NAFTA and the US hegemonic power, in view of the reinforcement of the other trading blocs.

The fact that Canada and Mexico want relations with Cuba means that a large slice of the extended North American economy wants it that way. The government of the US should follow the example of Mexico and Canada in relation to Cuba, not least because Cuba has an enormous geo-strategic value for North America, and because the Helms-Burton Law has been firmly rejected by most of its major trade partners. Should the US government decide to persist in the application of the Law, then the US would be acting very irresponsibly.

Inability to adapt to systemic changes is a clear sign of hegemonic decline; inability to provide leadership for its own regional integration group indicates lack of resolve.

It is time to hear the voices of the two other NAFTA countries and the international community. It is great time for the US to change. It is time to help Cuba to change.

Bibliography

Alponte, Juan María. **La Política Exterior de México en el Nuevo Orden Mundial**. México, FCE. 1993.

Brown, Craig (editor). **La Historia Ilustrada de Canadá.** México, FCE. 1994.

Brown, Seyom. **The Faces of Power** (2nd. ed.). Columbia University Press. 1994.

Canadiana (bimonthly leaflet of the Canadian Embassy in Mexico). Vol. 1, Num. 1. Mexico, June-July 1996.

Cuba Briefing Paper Series. Georgetown University. Several issues.

Dávila Villers, David R. (de.). **NAFTA, the First Year: a view from Mexico**. University Press of America. 1996.

Delacourt, Susan. **United We Fall**. Viking. 1993.

Dougherty, James E. and Robert L. Pfaltgraff, Jr. **American Foreign Policy**. Harper and Row. 1986.

E.U.A. **Instituto Mora** (10 vol.). Mexico, Instituto Mora. 1988.

Eduardo Galeano. **Las Venas Abiertas de América Latina**. Ed. Siglo XXI. 1977.

El Financiero [Mexico City newspaper]. Several issues.

García Reyes, Miguel & Ma. Gpe. López de Llergo. **Cuba después de la era soviética.** México, El Colegio de México. 1994.

IRELA (Institute for European-Latin American Relations). INF-96/1-CUB. **Cuba: ¿hacia una nueva crisis?**. Madrid, IRELA. March 3, 1996.

IRELA (Institute for European-Latin American Relations). INF-96/3-CUB. **Cuba y la Unión Europea: las dificultades del diálogo.** MADRID, IRELA. June 17, 1996.

Kegley, Jr., Charles W. and Eugene R. Wittkopf. **American Foreign Policy** (5th. ed.). Macmillan. 1996.

La Jornada [México City newspaper]. Several issues.

Latin American Monitor, Caribbean [Monthly Report]. London. Several issues.

McCormick, James M. American **Foreign Policy and Process** (2nd. ed.). Peacock. 1992.

Meyer, Lorenzo and Josefina Zoraida Vázquez. **The United States and Mexico.** The University of Chicago Press. 1985.

Morrison, Samuel E., Henry Steele C. y William E. Leuchtenburg. **Breve Historia de los Estados Unidos** (2nd. reprint). México, 1993.

NACLA. **Report on the Americas**. Several issues.

O'Neill, Jr., Thomas P. **Man of the House**. Random House. 1987.

Pellicer, Olga (editor). **Voz de México en la Asamblea General de la ONU**. México, FCE. 1994.

PROSPEL. **Anuario de Políticas Exteriores Latinoamericanas.** Several issues.

Revista Mexicana de Política Exterior (Mexico). Several issues.
Roett, Riordan (editor). **Relaciones Exteriores de México en la Década de los Noventa. Mexico, Siglo XXI.** 1991.
Rozental, Andrés. **La Política Exterior de México en la Era de la Modernidad.** Mexico. FCE. 1993.
Smith, Tony. **America's Mission.** Princeton University Press. 1994.
Solana, Fernando. **Cinco Años de Política Exterior.** Mexico. Porrúa. 1994.
Spanier, John. **La Política Exterior Norteamericana a Partir de la Segunda Guerra Mundial.** Buenos Aires, GEL. 1992.
The News [Mexico City newspaper]. Several issues.
Wilkerson, Loree A.R. **Fidel Castro's Political Program from Reformism to Marxism-Leninism**. University of Florida Press. 1965.
Wittkopf, Eugene R. **The Future of American Foreign Policy** (2nd. ed.). St. Martin's. 1994.

The Helms-Burton Affair
(a chronology[27])

2 May 1995	15 000 out of a total 22 000 Cuban refugees in Guantanamo will be allowed to enter the US. It was announced, on the other hand that the US would hereinafter send back all Cubans found in the sea.
19 May 1995	The entry into the US of the Guantanamo refugees and the forced return of the Cubans found in the sea was agreed by the two countries. The EU announced that it will maintain its humanitarian aid to Cuba for 1996.
23 May 1995	In Quito, the Group of Rio condemned, at a request from Mexico, the Helms-Burton project because it violates international law, the basic principles of regional understanding and the universal practices of free trade. This resolution will be sent to the US Congress and Executive. The Mexican Minister of Foreign Affairs declared that the "extra-territorial application of US law is unacceptable and it would constitute a dangerous international precedent."
6 July 1995	The Cuban GDP grew 0.7% (the figure had shrunk by 34.3% since 1989 when the Eastern Bloc collapsed). The 1994-95 zafra went down from the 4 million reported for 1993-94. However, Cuba received 1 314 million dollars in foreign currency during 1994. The commercial deficit amounted to 641 900 million dollars. Manufactures grew 7.6%, electricity, gas and water 4.4%, tourism 5.4%. Oil

	extraction exceeded the expectations for the first semester, amounting to 726 400 tons of crude. The target is set for 1.4 million tons at the end of the year.
12 July 1995	Viet Nam asked the US to end its economic blockade against Cuba. 36 Cubans arrived to Caracas from Guantanamo.
4 Sep 1995	The Castro government authorized Cuban exiles to invest in the island. The new investments law would allow foreigners to completely own enterprises in virtually all areas of the economy.
5 Sep 1995	There are 212 *mixed* enterprises with state participation in tourism, telecommunications an nickel.
20 Sep 1995	The US Secretary of State, Warren Christopher will send a recommendation for President Clinton to veto the Helms-Burton initiative.
21 Sep 1995	The House of Representatives approved the Helms-Burton initiative by landslide. More than 2/3 of the Chamber (67 Democrats and 227 Republicans) voted it before noon, after a failed Democratic attempt to delay the initiative. The vote (294 vs. 130) overrules the presidential veto.
18 Oct 1995	In Bariloche, Argentina, 19 heads of state of Latin America plus Spain and Portugal reject the US blockade against Cuba and showed "preoccupation" because of the Helms-Burton initiative. The Bariloche Declaration rejects such unilateral coercive measures that affect the well-being of the Iberoamerican peoples, run against free-trade, violate the sovereignty of the states, and run against the UN Charter, the World Trade Organization, the international law and the UN General Assembly.
17 Oct 1995	A minority group in the Senate delayed the approval of the Helms-Burton law for the second time in a week.
18 Oct 1995	Senator Jesse Helms made his proposal more flexible. The US issued Fidel Castro a visa to attend the UN 50th Anniversary celebration.
19 Jan 1996	Manuel Marín, the EC Vice-president for Latin America, said in Brussels that the EU maintains exploratory conversations with Cuba towards an economic cooperation agreement with the island.
9 Feb 1996	Negotiations between the EU and Cuba towards an economic cooperation agreement started in Havana.
24 Feb 1996	Cuban fighters down two civilian airplanes belonging to the anti-Castrite "Hermanos al Rescate."
27 Feb 1996	The UN Security Council approved early this morning a declaration "deploring" the shooting of the two civilian air-

	crafts and the likely killing of four persons. The UN asked the International Civil Aviation Organization a complete research on the incident. The US withdrew its initial "condemnation" for illegal use of force and threat to the international order, due to China's opposition.
28 Feb 1996	President Clinton and Congress agreed to escalate the blockade against Cuba, while the bilateral trade between Canada and the island exceeds the US 360 million per year.
4 Mar 1996	The US repatriates 5 Cubans more (in obedience of the May 1995 Agreement). 285 Cubans have been repatriated since the agreement was signed. In the same framework, 20 mil visas a year will be issued to Cubans wishing to emigrate to the US.
5 Mar 1996	The US Senate approves, by landslide (74 votes vs. 22) the Helms-Burton initiative. Canada and the CARICOM rejected the law as "extra-territorial" during a three day summit in Grenada, involving Jean Chrétian plus 14 heads of Caribbean states.
12 Mar 1996	President Clinton signs the Helms-Burton Law.
8 Jun 1996	President of the European Commission Jacques Santer announced president Clinton his discontent with the Helms-Burton law, that punishes foreign firms having business with Cuba.
6 July 1996	The main US industry and commerce associations aks president Clinton to suspend the application of title II of the Helms-Burton that allows law suits against foreign companies.
14 July 1996	The New York Times asks president Clinton to suspend title II of the "perverse" Helms-Burton law that confronts the US against Canada, the EU and Latin America.
16 July 1996	The EU is ready to apply countervailing measures against the law, including visa control on US businesspersons and the freezing of US assets. Nine executives of the Canadian mining company *Sherrit* and their families would be denied entry into the US. Others might soon, as well, receive similar treatment; among whom, executives of the Spanish hotel industry *SolMeliá* and the Italian company *Stet*. The same day, president Clinton adjourned title III of the Helms-Burton law to January 1997.
2 Oct 1996	The EU announces its decision to present a demand before the WTO against the Helms-Burton law. Canada, who would join the EU in such an effort, announced its decision to present a demand against the law in the framework of the NAFTA, as well.

4 Oct 1996	The EU deposed its demand against the Helms-Burton law before the WTO, the demand will be examined on 16 Oct.
18 Oct 1996	After the US objected (WTO countries can do it only once) the creation of a panel to analyze the European demand, the EU announced it will present it again on 20 Oct.
7 Nov 1996	European Union's trade commissioner Sir Leon Brittan is to present an important diplomatic initiative to mend diplomatic rifts between the US and the EU over Cuba.
20 Nov 1996	The WTO accepted to analyze the demand against the Helms-Burton law, presented by the EU and seconded by Canada and Mexico. A WTO panel will meet within 30 days, which will deliver a report in six months time.
20 Nov 1996	On returning to Havana, Fidel Castro announced that John Paul II will visit Cuba on 1997.
6 Dec 1996	In Brussels, Sir Leon Brittan informed the 15 European ministers of foreign affairs of his intention to demand not only the suspension but the cancellation of the Helms-Burton law, during a transatlantic summit between the EU and the US to be held on 16 Dec in Washington.
9 Dec 1996	On 9-14 Dec 1996, under the auspices of the Ford Foundation and led by Louis Frey Jr. (R. ex-Florida) and Toby Roth (R. Wisconsin), a group of congressmen and ex-congressmen visited Cuba and produced a report (delivered on January) to the US Congress and President: the US needs to re-define its Cuban policy because fidel Castro is not about to fall and he will not be ousted by the Helms-Burton law.
21 Dic 1996	Mexico and Canada join forces against the Helms-Burton. Both countries will support the EU demand against the law that is being analyzed by a WTO panel since 20 Nov 1996. Such position was made public at the end of the XII Ministerial Commission meeting between Lloyd Axworthy and José Angel Gurría.
25 Dec 1996	The Cuban legislature passed the *Law of Reaffirmation of Cuban Dignity and Sovereignty*, which allows Cubans to sue the US if they have been "victims of physical harm or property damage caused by actions supported by the US" including "murder, injury and economic damage suffered under torturers and assassins of the Batista dictatorship or criminals in the pay of North American imperialism." It also helps foreign companies to hide investments from US officials. Money sent to Cubans by relatives living abroad is tax-exempt and can be deposited in interest-bearing, hard-currency accounts in Cuba.

3 Jan 1997	President Clinton adjourned, for the second time, the title of the Helms-Burton that allows law suits against foreign companies.
28 Jan 1997	President Clinton announces an A.I.D. 800 million plan (title II of the Helms-Burton law) to assist Cuba should Fidel and Raúl leave. Castro replies that Cuba does not need donations buy the payment of the indemnities due to 34 years of economic blockade, in excess of 65 billion dollars.

Notes

1 The author is grateful to Alexis Juárez and Ariel Estévez for their help in preparing the present version of this paper.
2 Walter Hines Page, Woodrow Wilson's ambassador to Great Britain, in Smith, Tony. America's Mission. Princeton University Press. 1994. p. 60.
3 See Wilkerson, Loree A.R. Fidel Castro's Political Program from Reformism to Marxism-Leninism. University of Florida Press. 1965.
4 Seen in retrospective, the "Operation Mongoose" mounted by the CIA to murder Fidel Castro, seem taken from a James Bond manual (his food, his sea shells, his shoes, his cigars, etc).
5 The account of the Bay of Pigs fiasco, in April 1961, is to well known to be repeated. After the invasion, Cuba had "defeated the US imperialists." For the same reason, the October 1962 Missile Crisis story is not consigned here.
6 The failed assault to the Moncada (and subsequent imprisonment of Castro and followers) occurred on 26 July 1953.
7 Meyer, Lorenzo and Josefina Zoraida Vázquez. The United States and Mexico. The University of Chicago Press. 1985. p 178-179.
8 Until Jimmy Carter's "Human Rights policy."
9 Eduardo Galeano. Las Venas Abiertas de América Latina. Ed. Siglo XXI. 1977. p 116.
10 Cuba, of course, is not the only case in the world. We could cite Israel, El Salvador, even Europe under the Marshall Plan, etc.
11 Based on the Decreto Ley Número 50, issued on 15 February 1982, to promote "the economic association between Cuban and foreign entities."
12 Spain's new Prime Minister Asnar made a sudden turn in his country's foreign policy towards Cuba for which he was severely criticized within his country and in Latin American circles. Cuba denied its placet to the new Spanish ambassador in Havana. Bilateral relations are back to normal.
13 Imports plus exports, according to IMF-DOT Satatistics.
14 The Cuban Real GDP grew 0.7% in 1994; its GDP for 1995 is around 2.5%.
15 On 24th November 1992, the General Assembly approved a motion presented by the Cuban Delegation demanding an end to economic blockade against the island.
16 The first organization is led by Eloy Gutiérrez Menoyo who met with Chancellor Robaina in Madrid, on September 1994, and with Fidel Castro, in Havana, on June 1995. The second organization is led by Alfredo Durán, it is very active in Washington and is openly challenging the political influence of Más Canosa. Cf. NACLA, Report on the Americas, vol. XXIX, No. 2, Sep./Oct. 1995. p. 25.
17 IRELA. Cuba y la Unión Europea. INF-96/3-CUB. Madrid, IRELA. 17

Junio 1996. p 5.

18 *La Jornada* [Mexico City newspaper]. 13 July 1996. p 48.

19 Amendement to the Act on Foreign Extra-territorial Measures. Cfr. *Canadiana.* Canadian Embassy in Mexico City. Vol. 1, Num. 1. June-July 1996.

20 See chronology at the end of this paper; especially entries for October 1996, 20 November 1996 and 21 December 1996.

21 *Canadiana.* Op cit.

22 There are other Mexican investments in the island: hotels, concrete, etc.

23 Considering that two NAFTA countries (the US and Mexico) are the two most indebted in the world.

24 Not to be mistaken by the Ecu; which is used for commercial transactions only.

25 *La Jornada*, 3 February 1996. p 54. Spain is, of course, one of the main foreign investors in the island, as we have seen. For a discussion of the

26 NAFTA and its implications see Dávila Villers David R. (ed.). *NAFTA, the First Year: a View From Mexico.* University Press of America. 1996.

27 This chronology is taken mostly from several Mexican newspapers; chief among them, *La Jornada* and *El Financiero.*

www.ingramcontent.com/pod-product-compliance
Ingram Content Group UK Ltd.
Pitfield, Milton Keynes, MK11 3LW, UK
UKHW041102150926
475561UK00001BA/6

9 780761 810582